History Grounded

Looking for the History of Wales

About the author

Elin Jones has been interested in the history of Wales since her childhood, despite being taught little in school. But after gaining an MA in the history of England, she went on to complete an MA and a PhD in the history and literature of mediaeval Wales.

Years teaching history at Ysgolion Cyfun Preseli, Rhydfelen and Cwm Rhymni gave her experience in presenting her subject, and she found a different but very rich teaching environment when she became an Education Officer at the National Museum of Wales. After that, she was responsible for developing the history curriculum in Wales, and for a report on the Cwricwlwm Cymreig and the Story of Wales for the Welsh Government.

So, this book is the fruit of years of research and teaching, but the author emphasises that it is a personal journey through the history of Wales. The book reflects the author's interests and experiences, as all history books do. But she hopes you will enjoy reading it as much as she enjoyed writing it!

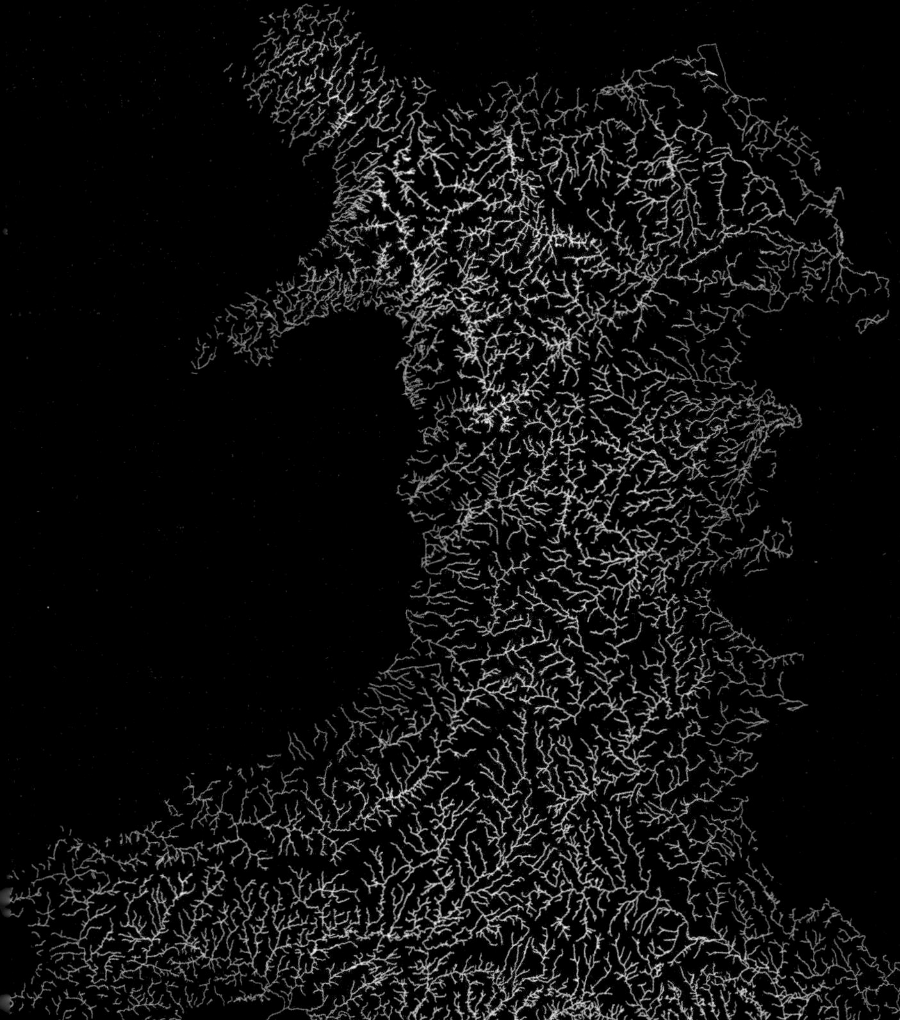

Names for the centuries

I have used the short forms 21C, 20C, 19C,18C to be clear and simple. Here are those short forms in words:

21C	twenty-first century
20C	twentieth century
19C	nineteenth century
18C	eighteenth century
17C	seventeenth century
16C	sixteenth century
15C	fifteenth century
14C	fourteenth century

Image on previous page:
a digital picture of the rivers of Wales

© Dafydd Elfryn

History Grounded

Looking for the History of Wales

Elin Jones

First edition: 2021
Reprinted: 2022
© text: Elin Jones
© publication: Gwasg Carreg Gwalch

All rights reserved. No part of this publication
may be reproduced, stored in a retrieval system,
or transmitted in any form or by any means, electronic, electrostatic, magnetic tape,
mechanical, photocopying, recording, or otherwise, without prior permission
of the authors of the works herein.

ISBN: 978-1-84527-832-8

Ariennir gan
Lywodraeth Cymru
Funded by
Welsh Government

Published with the financial support of the Welsh Government

Advisory panel:
Huw Griffiths, Eryl Owain, Toni Schiavone, Hedd Ladd Lewis
Director: Myrddin ap Dafydd
Manager: Llio Elenid
Trialled by teachers at:
Ysgol Bethel, Gwynedd; Ysgol Glantaf, Caerdydd;
Ysgol Gynradd Penparc, Ceredigion; Ysgol Cwm Banwy, Powys.
Text editor: Marian Beech Hughes
Picture research and photographs: Iestyn Hughes
Images for the cover: Elin Manon
Cover design: Dylunio GraffEG
Inside pages design: Dylunio GraffEG

Published by Gwasg Carreg Gwalch,
12 Iard yr Orsaf, Llanrwst, Wales LL26 0EH tel: 01492 642031
email: books@carreg-gwalch.cymru
website: www.carreg-gwalch.cymru

Printed and published in Wales

This book is dedicated to Josephine

HISTORY GROUNDED

Introduction

I'd like to have a time machine and go back through the centuries, to see what things were like in those far-off days. BUT – we can't travel back in time, not to last year, nor yesterday – not even to the second you started to read this sentence. We can remember, we can tell a story, we can look at a photograph – but we can't relive the past. It has slipped like water through our fingers.

The author, Elin Jones, at the door of the little church at Ffynnon Fair, Penrhys, Rhondda

But we can see the marks the past has left. We can see it in our homes. There's the crack in the window after a game of football, or the scratches on the door that remind us how keen the dog is to go for a walk. Maybe there are marks on a wall somewhere in your house that show how you've grown – and that's a bit of your history that's now part of the history of your home too.

The past leaves its mark on us too. That's what a suntan is. And do you have a scar on your knee after you fell off your bike?

There are lots of old photograph albums in people's homes. Open one, ask who the people were and listen to the stories about them ...

HISTORY GROUNDED

For centuries, people have been collecting stories and legends in books. These can tell us about our past.

People have lived on this planet for thousands and thousands and thousands of years, and they have left their mark on almost every part of it. When we find the things made by people who lived here in the past, the evidence for their lives, we start to find out the history of a country.

```
Look at the place names where you live. Find a
   map showing the villages, the rivers and the
   hills. Many of these will be Welsh names - the
            language belongs to us all.
```

Some people think you can only find out about the past by reading books. But you can find out about it too by looking around you wherever you are. The buildings you see and the names of towns, and their streets as well – they have all got something to tell us about the past.

This book will help you to find out about history wherever you are in Wales.

But how do we know about the past anyway?

Because, for hundreds of years, people have wanted to know about it! They would pass on stories they had heard from their parents. Some mountains look like a 'giant's chair' – and perhaps the name of an old hero is kept alive in the mountain's name. Sometimes there is an old name on a standing stone or a big rock in the ground.

Then people began to write things down. This happened at different times and in different countries, from Egypt to China and Guatemala. Once people had begun to write, they began to keep records and note important happenings. Later they began to write books, sometimes about their own past.

Today, we study the things made by people in the past, and the things they have written. Some people look specially for things made in the past which have ended up in the earth under our feet. We call these people archaeologists. Others specialise in the history written in books – they are historians. But archaeologists and historians depend on each other to get a better picture of the past. By today they also depend on the

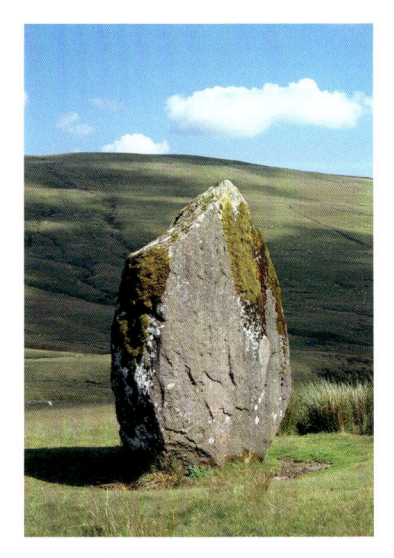

Maen Llia in the Brecon Beacons. Thousands of years ago, people must have worked hard to raise this huge stone ... But nobody knows why. That story has been lost by now.

HISTORY GROUNDED

Archaeologists and volunteers digging in the earth on a site at Dinas Dinlle, near Caernarfon; (below) an archaeologist holding part of a knife made about a thousand years ago

work of scientists. They use science and technology to find traces of the past. Then they can study it in detail. Scientists today have amazing skills. They can use machines to find in the ground the shape of a building which vanished from sight centuries ago. Or they can find the original colour of the wallpaper in an old house. By putting someone's tooth in a special machine, scientists can find out a lot about that person's health, their food and their childhood. The latest developments in genetics mean we can trace someone's family back into the distant past.

HISTORY GROUNDED

Yr Ysgwrn was the home of the poet Hedd Wyn, who was killed in battle in 1917. The house was restored in 2017. When the wallpaper was being scraped off in one room, 26 layers of paper were found there! Each one was from a different time – and each one would have had its story.

But although we have all this technology, and all this knowledge too, we still have to GUESS. The more knowledge you have, the better your guesses are, but we can't – yet – go back into the past.

This book uses the knowledge and the ideas of all these people. But decisions have to be made what to put in it, and what to leave out. So, this is ONE story about Wales, and about what you can learn by visiting its towns, villages, beaches and hills.

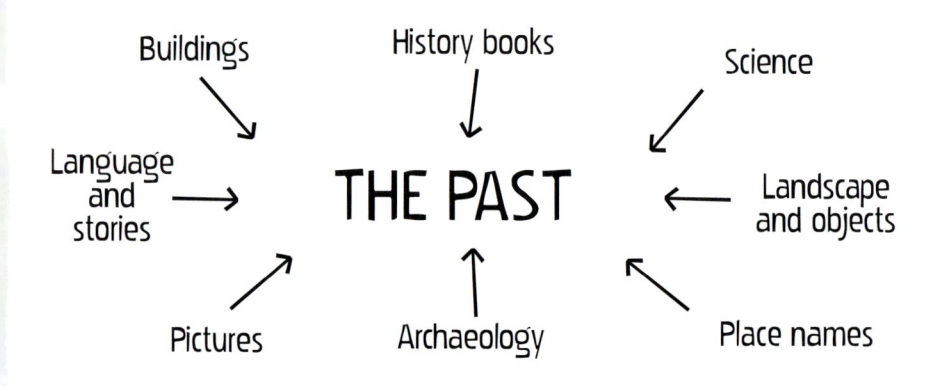

Buildings → THE PAST ← Science
History books ↓
Language and stories →
↑ Pictures   ↑ Archaeology   ↑ Place names
Landscape and objects →

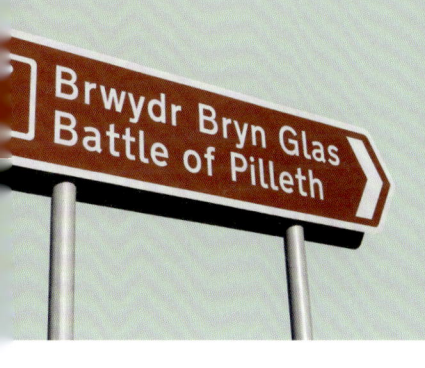

The site of Owain Glyndŵr's great victory at Pilleth, Radnorshire, Powys, in 1402. You can walk across the battlefield today and see what an advantage the Welsh had from being at the top of a steep hill. There is a fence around the tall trees on the slope. According to one story, the bodies of hundreds of dead soldiers were buried there – but you can't see any sign of that on the ground today.

First warning

I'm afraid there's a lot of death and war and cruelty in history. People who are kind and get on with each other don't leave much for us to find. People who kill each other, leaving bones and weapons buried in the ground, and people who build tombs for the dead and forts and castles to defend themselves – these are the people who leave their mark on a country. As time goes on, it gets better – but not much.

HISTORY GROUNDED

Second warning

Once people began to write things down, about 3,000 to 4,000 years ago, it's easier to find out what was happening to them. Before that, for thousands and thousands of years, we know almost nothing about how people lived. Probably, it didn't change much for thousands of years. But things were happening, and changing too – very, very slowly. We have to GUESS a lot about long ago history.

And we must remember too that all history is written by people who have learnt how to write – and have got the time to sit down to put pen to paper. For centuries and centuries many more boys than girls learnt to read, write and count. So, it was men who wrote history and, unfortunately, they preferred to write the history of men too!

Sometimes we come across a piece of old newspaper in an old cupboard. Maybe it's only a few years old, but it looks so different. We might recognise some of the names in it, or some of the places in the photographs. But, for thousands of years, all books had to be written by hand. This is a book about the history of Wales written 800 years ago, and on goatskin, not paper! Imagine how hard it is to follow.

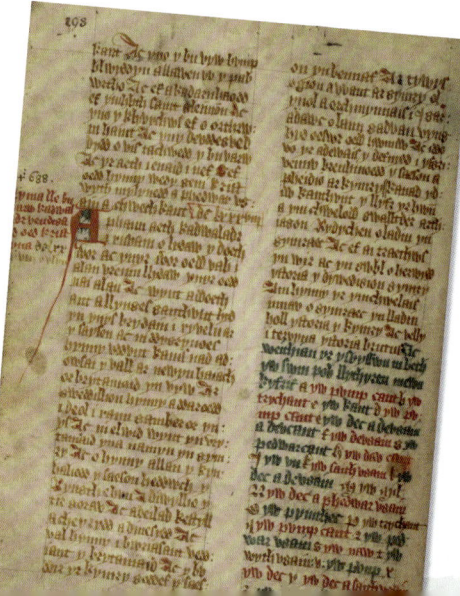

HISTORY GROUNDED

Shirley Bassey singing to members of the Bute Street Rainbow Club, Cardiff, in 1957. The Rainbow Club was a typical youth club in the area and its members' families originally came from all parts of the world. It's worth watching films like *A Stroll Through Tiger Bay* on YouTube.

Over the centuries people from all parts of the world have come to all parts of Wales - and they brought their stories with them to weave into the history of Wales. You can see what a rich mixture of cultures there is in Wales now when you go to Ysgol Gynradd Gymraeg Hamadryad in Cardiff. The pupils (in 2021) come from homes where 22 different languages are spoken, including Welsh and English.

HISTORY GROUNDED

Workers chatting over a cuppa. We can only guess what they were talking about. Poor wages, perhaps ... the dangers of their work ... local sports teams ... politics and religion ... or the latest bit of gossip ... they are telling stories ...

Apprentices in a weapons factory in Cardiff during the Second World War. They're telling stories too!

Although very many countries have a long, rich history, if it wasn't written down, almost all of it will have been lost. We have to try to find it by looking for the things we can see in those countries – the things people have made, artefacts like pots, pictures, jewellery and statues.

This all means that history has been written by men, and most of these men had white skins and lived in Europe. They wrote about men like themselves too. We have to remember this all the time when we are trying to find out about the past.

Elin Jones
Summer 2021

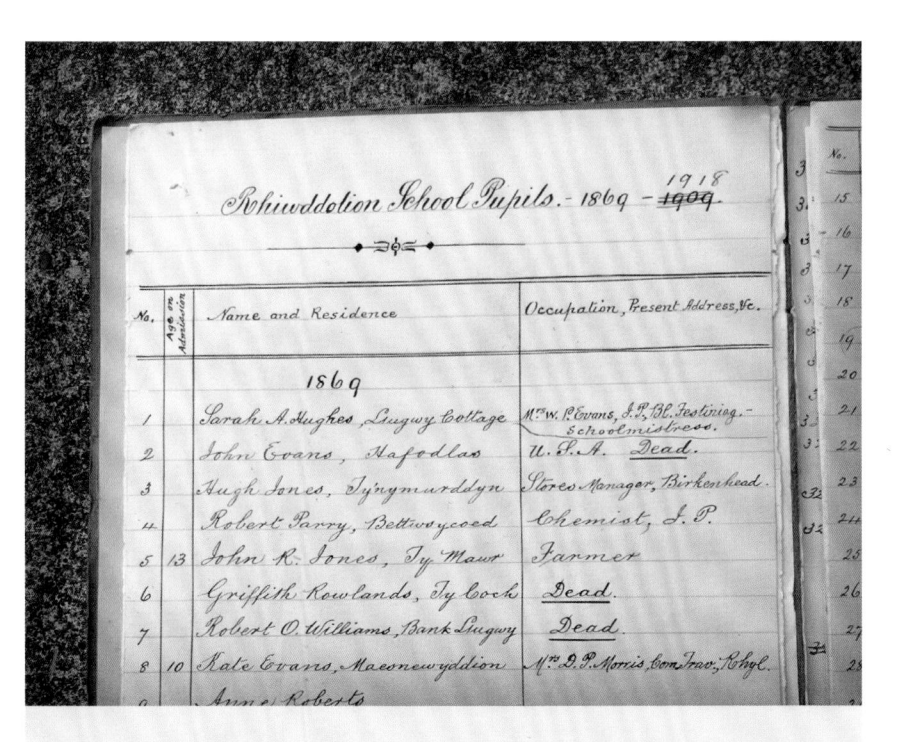

And what about the stories of Welsh children? School record books tell us a lot about education in the past. This is from the records of Ysgol Rhiwddolion, near Betws-y-coed. The village is just a ruin now, but this list tells us about the lives - and the language - of the past.

HISTORY GROUNDED

Cromlech
about -3500

Hillfort
about -1300 to 50

Roman fort
about 70 to 400

Dates

Part 1: Timeline

Questions

- Who were the first people to live here?
- Where can you hear Celtic languages spoken today?

HISTORY GROUNDED

| Church about 500 | Offa's Dyke about 780 | The Laws of Hywel Dda about 930 |

- How did the Romans leave their mark on the country?
- Why was Christianity so important in Wales?
- What happened after the Romans left?

This picture shows what is left of a 5,000 year-old forest. It was covered over when the sea level rose as the ice sheet of the Ice Age thawed. But these tree stumps on the beach at Borth, Ceredigion, sometimes appear again after storms.

These trunks and roots remind us of the tale of Cantre'r Gwaelod – one of the most popular legends of Wales. When we use the word 'tale' today, it means a made-up story. But before people could write, people and events from the past were remembered by telling stories about them. As the story was told and re-told, it would change and become bigger and more dramatic. This always happens when people tell stories, even about things that have happened to them. Think of how you tell your friends about the things that have happened to you. Have you ever 'improved' the bare details of a story?

CAVES AND CROMLECHI
The very first people

The story of human beings goes back at least 300,000 years. For most of that long time we believe people lived like animals, hunting other animals – and being hunted by animals themselves. They didn't leave their mark on the places they lived, and if they built anything like houses, none have been found. They probably lived in caves or sheltered in them. As time went on, they began to make tools of stone and bone. Archaeologists have found the bones and tools of some of these early people. They can begin to find out about them and the way they lived by taking these things to a museum and studying them.

The entrance to Pontnewydd Cave, near St Asaph

A hand axe from Cadfarch, Powys

But there's nothing to be seen now in the places where these early people lived.

In Pontnewydd Cave, near St Asaph, archaeologists found the jawbone and a few teeth of a child who was about nine years old when he or she died – about 230,000 years ago. There were over a thousand different bits of stone in the cave too. The people who lived there would hit one piece of stone against another to make a kind of hammer or knife.

Thousands and thousands of years went by, and people were learning to make better tools of stone and bone. Perhaps they had wooden ones too, but those would have rotted away and disappeared. They got food to eat by hunting animals and gathering plants, fruit and seeds.

About 5,000 years ago, the first really big change happened. That's when people learnt how to make and use fire and how to plant and look after crops. They made beautiful tools of polished stone too, and used tiny, sharp pieces of stone for the heads of arrows and spears. These changes took a long, long time to happen, and at different times in every part of the world.

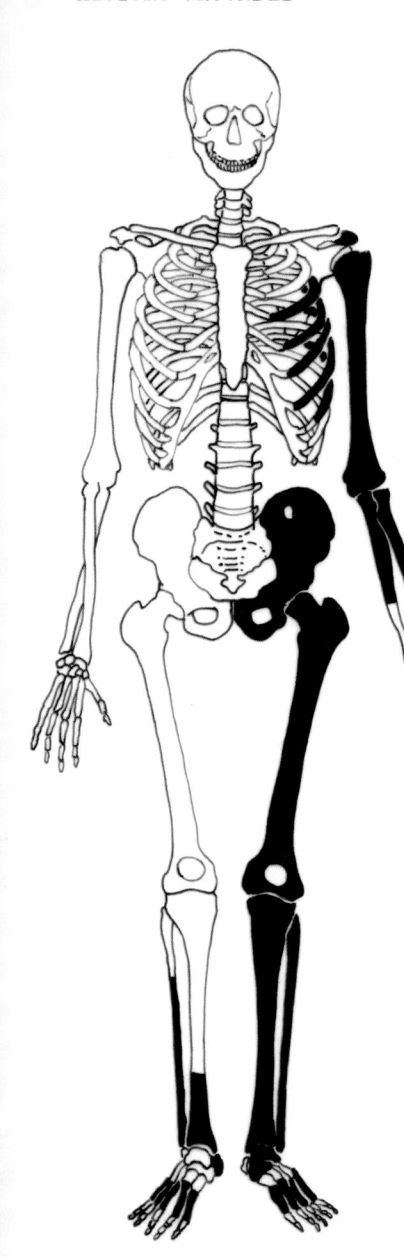

The 'black' bones in this picture come from Paviland Cave

HISTORY GROUNDED

The steep, rough cliff on Gower where the mouth of Paviland Cave faces the sea: the sea level was higher centuries ago. Detail: inside the cave

These were the first people to leave any mark on Wales, by cutting down trees and ploughing the land. They would cut down or burn the forests to clear the ground to plant crops. Then, when the crops began to fail, they would move on to clear a new piece of ground. If you look at the bare hills of Wales today, you can see the marks these first farmers made. Over thousands of years, they destroyed the forests to farm the land, leaving the land on the hills poor and sour. No forests would grow there again.

But these same people made some amazing things too. They managed to build *cromlechi* – one truly enormous stone that sits on top of three or four other huge stones that have been put to stand upright in the ground. No-one really knows how they did it.

A stone axe-head made at Graig Lwyd, Penmaen-mawr

Bare hills near Llyn y Fan Fach

HISTORY GROUNDED

The map shows where in Wales you can see the most important cromlechi (left), stone circles and standing stones (right). You can see that they seem to follow the main valleys, and archaeologists think they may have been made by people who came over the sea from the west and travelled up the main valleys.

Some of the cromlechi and ancient stones of Wales

Bryn Cader Faner, Meirionnydd

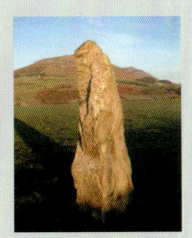

Maen Penfras Uchaf, near Pwllheli

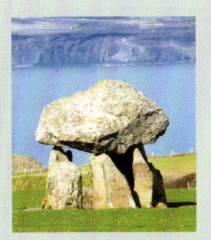

Carreg Samson, Pembrokeshire

Pentre Ifan, Pembrokeshire

Din Llugwy, Anglesey

Tinkinswood, Vale of Glamorgan

25

The stone circle above Penmaen-mawr, Conwy

When they were first built, each cromlech would have been covered over with earth, and some still are. Each cromlech was a grave, but it may have been a meeting place too. Nobody really knows. It is so long ago that nobody remembers, and the people who built these amazing things didn't write. There are nearly 150 cromlechi in Wales, and hundreds more in Ireland, Scotland, Spain and Brittany.

The people who made the cromlechi also built huge circles of stones or wood, like Stonehenge. That is in England, but some of the stones there come from the Preseli hills, nearly two hundred miles away. Nobody knows how those enormous stones were taken to Stonehenge either, nor why it was built. But there are lots of different explanations for it. We still have to GUESS!

Stonehenge, Wiltshire, England

HILLFORTS

The Iron Age

About 3,000 years ago some people began to make things out of the metal ore that is in some stones. At first, they used metals which are easy to melt and to shape – especially copper and tin. Iron is harder

A recreation of a Celtic village, built by interpreting archaeological evidence. This is on the site of a hillfort at Castell Henllys, Pembrokeshire.
Detail: the sword from Llyn Fawr

to work, but things made of iron are much harder and sharper than ones made of copper or bronze (tin and copper mixed). The oldest thing made of iron which has been found in Wales was in Llyn Fawr, above the Rhondda Valley. It was made about 2,600 years ago. It is part of a sword. Perhaps it was made in Wales, but no one knows for certain.

Writing

By this time, people in other parts of the world, like Greece and Egypt, had begun to live in towns. They were making beautiful buildings to live in – and they were writing too. They wrote books

Round house, Holyhead Mountain, Anglesey

about mathematics, science, geography and history. Because they were written down, there are lots of poems and plays from Greece for to us to enjoy today. This is why we know so much about Greeks and Egyptians, even though they lived so long ago.

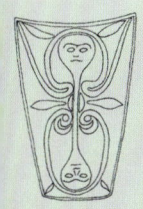

A collection of pieces of tools and Celtic art from the Iron Age was found at Tal-y-llyn, Meirionnydd. One special piece shows two faces joined by one neck. It must have had an important meaning to the person who made it: what do you think that might have been? This drawing of it was made by John Meirion Morris, and he thinks it shows an image of the circle of life, which was important to the Celts.

The Celts

But place names as well as buildings and tools can tell us about the past. About 3,000 years ago the Greeks wrote a lot about people they called Celts who lived near them. According to the Greeks, these Celts lived all over Europe. They spoke a different language. This language was perhaps the ancestor of the Welsh we talk today, and the ancestor too of Breton, Cornish, Scots Gaelic, Manx and Irish. There are lots of place names in Europe, from France, Germany and Spain, and as far as Turkey, which come from this old language.

The Greeks said that the Celts loved fighting, and that it was very important to them to be brave in battle. The Celtic word for that bravery was *gâl*. And that word is part of place names like Galicia in Spain and Galatia in Turkey. Gaul, the old name for France, comes from the same word.

We do know that the Celts were very skilful craftspeople, because the jewellery and tools that survive from their time are so beautifully made. We can see some of the lovely things they made in museums across in Europe. Some of these had patterns on them which seem to change shape as you look at them.

But we must also remember that the Celts, like the other people of this time, used slaves. One of the masterpieces of Celtic ironwork was discovered in Llyn Cerrig Bach, Anglesey. It was a chain to tie a group of slaves together by their necks.

A lot of what we know about them comes from books written by the people who fought against them – the people of Greece and Rome. There is still a lot we have to GUESS about them, remembering that people don't often say good things about their enemies.

HISTORY GROUNDED

Place names across Europe come from the language of the Celts

- Scotland — Dundee
- Belhaven (bala)
- The Isle of Man
- Ireland — Dundalk
- Beltough (Bala)
- Y Bala
- Dinas Emrys
- Dinmore
- Wales
- Cornwall
- Brittany
- Dover (waters)
- Verdun
- Balaton
- Balat
- Bala Bala
- Galicia
- River Dubra (water)
- Dunbria
- River Douro (water)

■ The birthplace of Celtic culture   ■ Areas of Europe influenced by the Celts

29

HISTORY GROUNDED

Hillforts

You can see the ruins of the Celts' homes in hillforts across Europe, wherever the Celts lived. A hillfort is a collection of houses built on top of a high hill. There are ditches and banks of earth all round these houses. There are over 600 hillforts in Wales. Because hillforts are built in places that are difficult to get to, and well defended, they were probably meant to be safe places for people to shelter during wars. But there's not much to prove that, because very few things have been found in the hillforts except the foundations of houses.

Pen-y-crug, near Brecon (above), and a drawing of what a Celtic village may have looked like on Holyhead Mountain, Anglesey

Picture opposite: Tre'r Ceiri hillfort, Llŷn. The small circles inside the walls are the foundations of houses. Detail: the remains of one of the houses

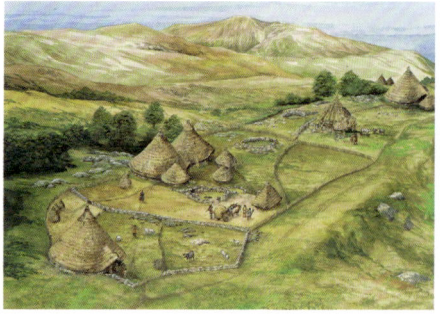

30

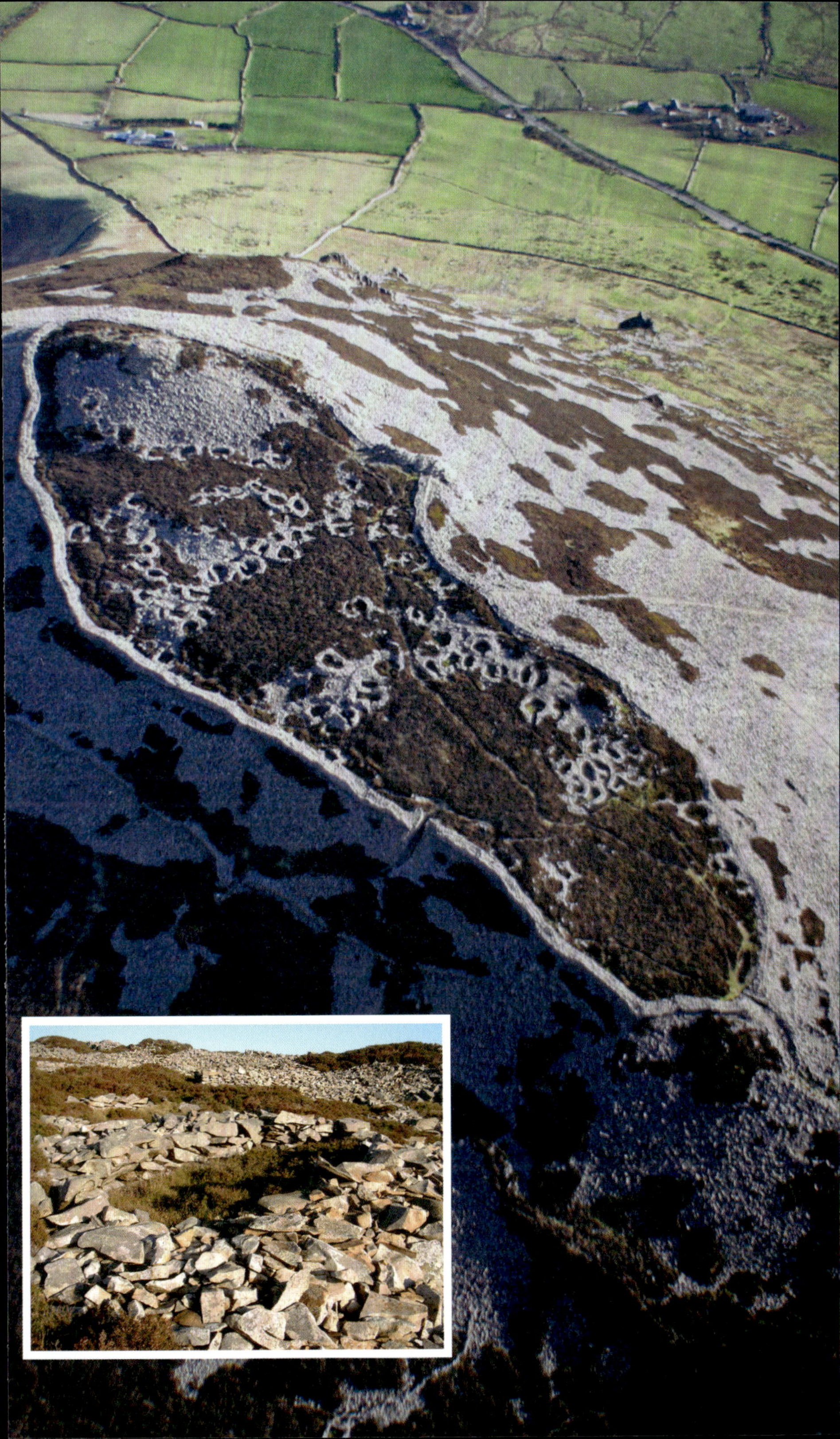

Caerwent, Caerleon, Caerfyrddin – many of our towns combine Celtic and Latin elements in their names.

The Romans

Although the Greeks fought with the Celts, they didn't try to conquer them. But about 2,000 years ago the people of one town in Italy started to try to conquer the other towns around them. The name of that town was Rome,

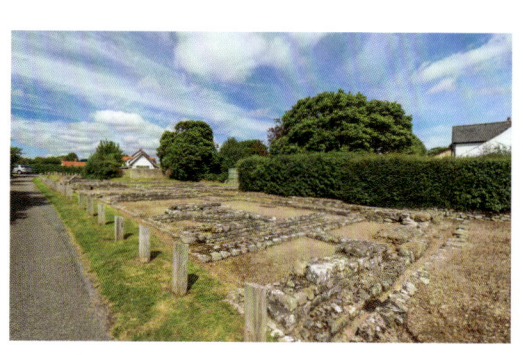

Above is part of the Roman wall of Caerwent and a row of shops in this amazing town

and over the centuries it built an empire which stretched from Scotland to north Africa, and from Spain to the borders of Iran.

The Romans left their mark on every part of Europe. For over 1,000 years their language, Latin, was the language of education everywhere in Europe. When Constantine, one of the Roman emperors, decided to become a Christian, Christianity became the official religion of the whole empire. The Pope is still the head of one group of Christians – the Roman Catholic church. He still lives in the old city of Rome.

HISTORY GROUNDED

The Roman fort of Segontium – a part of the town of Caernarfon today

33

HISTORY GROUNDED

Part of the barracks for the legionary soldiers who were based in Caerleon, the Romans' biggest fort in Wales

It was through fighting that the Romans won all the countries that they ruled. Their soldiers were very disciplined, and their army well organised. For example, every Roman fort was built to exactly the same pattern. This meant that every soldier would always know where to find the headquarters, the weapon store, the offices and all the other buildings. If you look at the pattern of the Roman fort in Segontium, near Caernarfon, or Caerleon, near Newport, you will see that they are on exactly the same plan as a Roman fort in Spain, north Africa or Turkey.

Every Roman soldier had to be able to walk 30 kilometres a day, carrying all his weapons and his equipment on his back. The Romans built good roads to connect every part of their empire – and all those roads led to Rome.

HISTORY GROUNDED

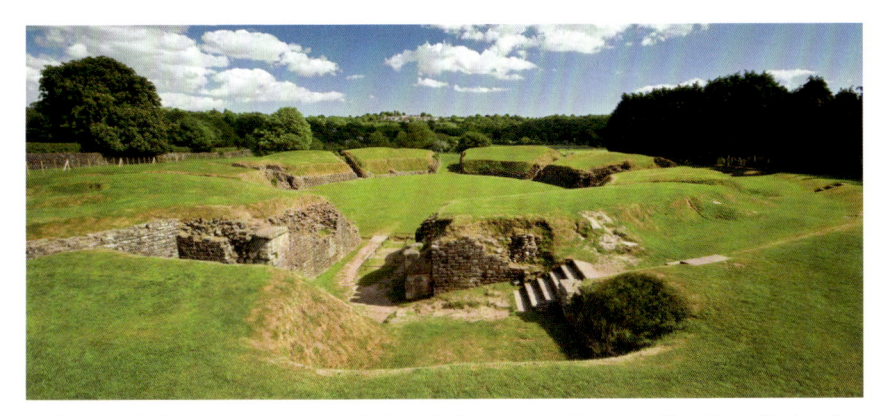

The amphitheatre in Caerleon (above); the Roman baths at Caerleon (below)

You can see clearly the square corners of the Roman fort at Tomen y Mur, Trawsfynydd. The mound was built there afterwards in the Middle Ages.

HISTORY GROUNDED

FORTS, TOWNS AND ROADS

On the map opposite and in some of the pictures that come after it, you can see where the Roman forts were in Wales, and what they were like. The forts were the homes of the Roman soldiers. There was a big fort in Caernarfon, Gwynedd, and an even bigger one in Caerleon, Gwent, over 250 kilometres away. These two forts are quite different to the hillforts. There was a network of roads and smaller forts between them.

CAER

The word *caer* belongs to the Celtic languages. It's a form of the words *cae* ("field") and "close", as in "I close the door". It's an old word for a safe place, a defended enclosure. Often this means walls which protect the heart of the institution. Most of the Roman remains in Wales are military ones – the roads and the forts. Many of these forts grew into towns and those still include the element *caer* in the place name. The picture above is of the village of Caerwent, which is still surrounded by walls of the old Roman town. The Celtic hillforts had rounded walls, or ones that curved to follow the shape of the land, but the Romans built straight walls and square corners.

HISTORY GROUNDED

The main Celtic tribes in Wales in Roman times and the main Roman centres

Map showing tribes and Roman centres in Wales:

Tribes: DECEANGLI, ORDOVICES, CORNOVII, DEMETAE, SILURES

Locations and features:
- x copper (north coast)
- copper x
- lead x
- Holyhead
- Canovium (Caerhun)
- Deva (Chester) □
- Segontium (Caernarfon)
- x copper
- Tomen y Mur
- Caer-gai
- copper/lead x
- Viroconium (Wroxeter) □
- Pennal
- Llanfair Caereinion
- lead x
- Caersŵs
- Crosswood
- Llanio
- Castell Collen
- Dolaucothi (gold) x
- Y Gaer
- Gobannium (Abergavenny)
- Maridunum (Carmarthen)
- Nidum (Neath)
- Burrium (Usk)
- Gelligaer
- Isca (Caerleon) □
- iron x
- x lead
- Cardiff
- Venta Silurum (Caerwent)

Legend:
- □ A legionary fortress
- • Minor forts, with Roman roads connecting them
- x Mines

SCALE: 20 miles / 32 km

A stone marking the grave of one of the Ordovices at Penbryn, Ceredigion

37

Two Celts

Caradog (Caratacus)

When the Romans first began to attack Britain, Caradog (Caratacus to the Romans) was king of most of the south of Britain. He won victories against them, and this was reason the Roman emperor Claudius said he had to invade Britain in AD43. Although Caradog won more battles against the Roman armies, he was defeated in the end. He escaped to the west, and became the leader of two tribes, the Silures and the Ordovices, before he lost one last battle.

He escaped again, going north this time to the Brigantes. But this time their queen, Cartimandua, gave Caradog up to the Romans. He, his wife and his children were taken as prisoners to Rome. There, according to the Roman historian Tacitus, Caradog made such a dignified and brave speech to the Emperor that he decided to spare his life, and to treat him with respect. So Caradog and his family were given an honourable home in Rome — but they were never allowed to go back home to Britain.

The Silures, a Celtic tribe, lived in Glamorgan and Gwent. This is an artist's impression of what one of their warriors might have looked like. According to Tacitus, a Roman historian, these were the bravest and fiercest warriors the Romans had ever fought. They were guerrilla fighters when Caradog came to them after losing his kingdom in the east.

The story of Caradog has inspired many generations. This is an artist's interpretation of Caradog facing the Roman emperor.

Caer Caradog on the borders of Wales, one of the several possible sites of Caradog's last battle

An artist has imagined how Boudicca and her daughters might have looked leading their army in the rebellion of the Iceni and the Trinovantes against the Romans in the year 60

Buddug (Boudicca)

The Romans believed strongly that girls and women of every age belonged to men – first to their fathers, then to their husbands once they married. The Celts had queens as well as kings as their leaders, and the Romans thought that was very wrong and unnatural. One of these queens was Buddug, which means "victory" (the name was Boudica or Boudicca in Celtic and Boadicea sometimes in English). She and her husband led the Iceni tribe in the south-east of Britain, and they had accepted being ruled by the Romans. But when Buddug's husband died in AD61, the Romans took her and her daughters and abused them in public. Buddug decided to take revenge on the Romans, and led her people to a series of victories. She captured and destroyed several of the Roman towns the Romans had built, including Londinium (London today). But Buddug and her people were defeated in the end when the Romans turned the full force of their legions against her. According to one story, Buddug killed herself rather than be taken a prisoner by the Romans.

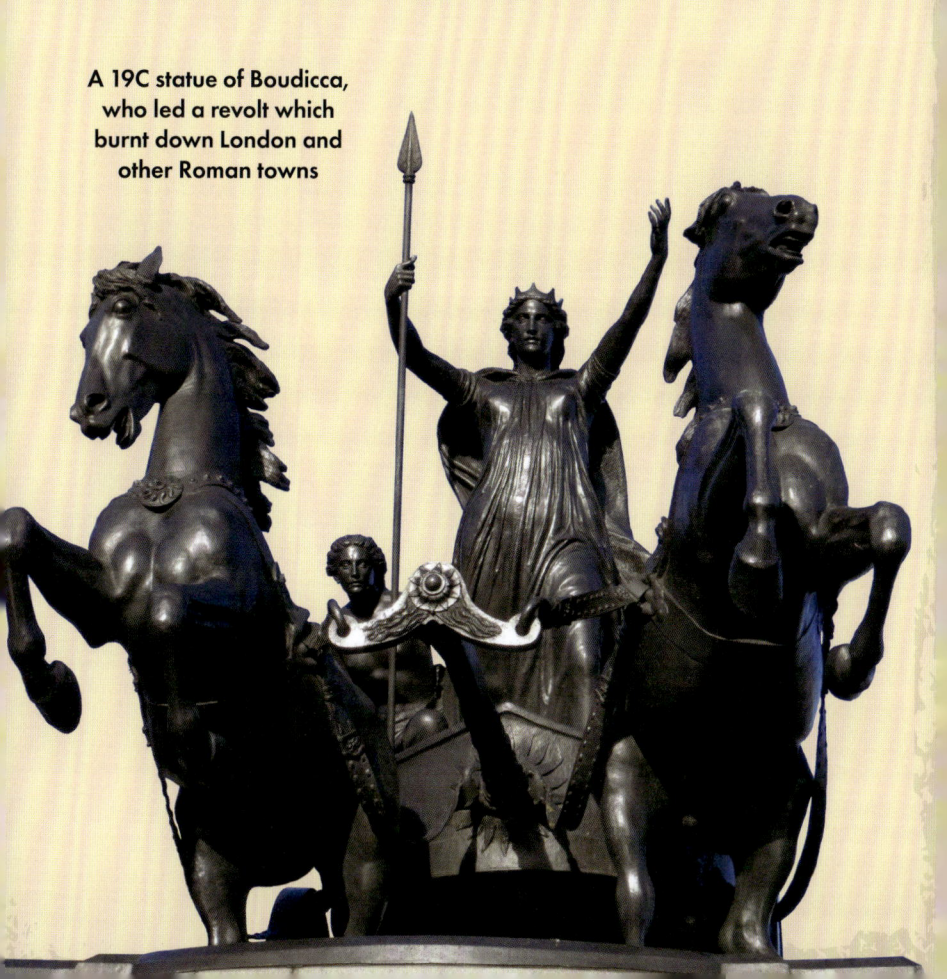

A 19C statue of Boudicca, who led a revolt which burnt down London and other Roman towns

HISTORY GROUNDED

Part of Sarn Elen crossing Hirfynydd to the north of the Neath Valley.

These holes at the bottom of the cliff at the Great Orme, Llandudno, are an ancient entrance to the copper mines

The Romans in Wales

You can still see the ruins of some Roman forts, towns and houses. You can see the remains of their roads too, although many of these have disappeared under roads built over them afterwards. People carried on using the Roman roads for centuries. Parts of a Roman road between Aberconwy and Carmarthen are still called "Sarn Elen" today, after a legendary Roman empress from Wales. These roads were well paved and drained, and they were still being used to link different parts of Wales together a thousand years after they were built.

Some towns in Wales today follow the pattern of the Roman towns too. You can't see a single Roman building in Carmarthen today. But if you stand in front of the council offices, which are on the site of the headquarters of the Roman town, and walk from there to the most important church in Carmarthen, you will be walking in the footsteps of the Romans. The church was built on the site of the temple of Jupiter, the most important of the Roman gods.

The Romans opened lots of mines in Wales, using slaves to do the dangerous and dirty work of digging for the valuable metals in the earth. These mines were in every part of Wales, from the copper mines on the Great Orme, above Llandudno, to the iron mines on the Little Garth, Glamorgan, and from the lead mines of Flintshire to the gold mines of Dolaucothi in Carmarthenshire.

The Romans left their mark on the Welsh language, and on many

HISTORY GROUNDED

The Roman Legionary Museum, Caerleon, which was built to look like a Roman temple

other European languages, like Spanish and French. Books probably first came to Britain with the Romans. That explains words like *llyfr* (*book* in Welsh), which comes from the Latin *librum*, and *ysgrifen* (writing) from the Latin *scribendum*. But sometimes we just can't work out why people in Britain chose to use Latin words instead of words in their own language. We can only scratch our heads, because the words for *pen* (head), *llaw* (hand) and *troed* (foot) come from the Celtic, but the words for *corff* (body), *braich* (arm) and *coes* (leg) come from Latin. Hundreds of other Welsh words came from Latin too, like *pont* (bridge), *porth* (door), *mur* (wall) and *ffenest* (window). The Celtic Brythonic language changed into Welsh in towns like Caerwent and in the little villages that grew up around the Roman forts, where the soldiers' families lived.

A copy of a Roman milestone. This stone was found at Bwlch y Ddeufaen ("the gap with two stones") between the Conwy Valley and the Menai Strait.

HISTORY GROUNDED

EARLY CHRISTIAN CHURCHES

The Romans were pagans to begin with, worshipping a lot of different gods, like the people of the other countries they conquered. The Romans were ready to let people worship their own gods, as long as they all accepted that the emperor was one of the gods and made sacrifices to him. But Jews and Christians refused to do that, and so they were persecuted.

Then, in AD313, the emperor Constantine announced an end to the persecution, and allowed the Christians and Jews to worship their God publicly. At the end of his life Constantine was baptised a Christian. From then on, Christianity was the official religion of the Empire.

Christianity has left its mark on Wales, on its language and on its culture too. Nobody knows how or when Christianity came to Britain. But it must have happened before Constantine was emperor, because it seems that three men were martyred – killed because of their faith – two of them, Julius and Aaron, in Caerleon.

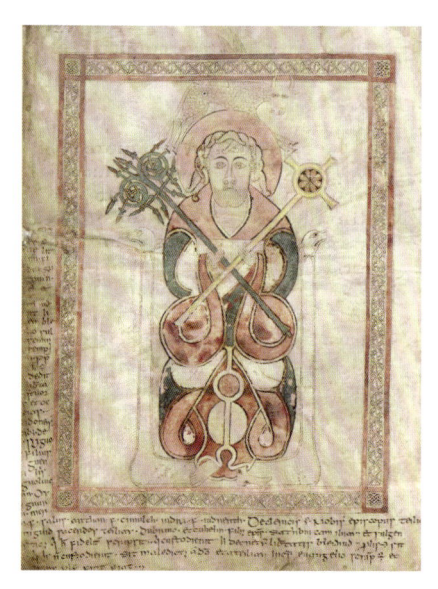

The Book of Teilo. This was one of the treasures of Llandeilo church, but it was taken from there and is now kept at Lichfield Cathedral. Sometimes, museums in Wales have been allowed to borrow it.

From Roman times on, Wales was a Christian country, even after Rome's power came to an end in the 5C, when many countries in Europe went back to worshipping pagan gods.

It's possible that some people in Wales continued to be pagans too. But because it was churchmen who kept the records and wrote the history from now on, their version of history is the only one we have.

An example of an early "llan" – Llanfaglan church on the shores of Menai Strait, near Caernarfon

Welsh saints

We don't know a lot about Wales in the centuries after the Romans. It was a troubled time, when people fought amongst themselves. Pagans from the north and the east of Europe attacked the empire and the Romans could no longer defend it. To begin with, these attackers would take people's belongings, take some of them for slaves and burn down homes. Then they began to make their own homes here when they realised the Roman legions weren't coming back. Because of this, there aren't many buildings from this time to be seen today.

Many of the Welsh saints who have given their names to so many of our towns and villages belong to these violent centuries. A person who

HISTORY GROUNDED

St Trillo's Chapel, Llandrillo-yn-Rhos, which was built over a holy spring in the 16C

tried to live according to their faith, who preached and helped people in need was called a saint. Many of our towns and villages are named after saints. The word *llan* means a piece of ground with a wall or fence round it. Because a church would always be in a *llan*, the word came to mean "the site of a church", although it has kept its original meaning in words like *perllan* (orchard) and *gwinllan* (vineyard). A church would be linked to a particular saint (or saints), sometimes because they had built the first church there, or

Maen Beuno (St Beuno's Stone) at Clynnog Fawr church

The Great Cross of Nevern, or St Brynach's Cross, from the 9C or 10C. Perhaps it was there in the time of Hywel Dda.

46

HISTORY GROUNDED

Early Churches and Monasteries

- Holyhead †
- † Penmon
- † Bangor
- † Abergele
- † Llanynys
- † Clynnog Fawr
- Bangor-on-Dee †
- Bardsey †
- † Aberdaron
- † Meifod
- † Tywyn
- † Llandinam
- Llanbadarn †
- † Llangurig
- † Saint Harmon
- Glasgwm †
- † Llanddewibrefi
- Glasbury †
- † St David's
- † Llandeilo Fawr
- † Llanarthne
- Henllan †
- † Penalun
- † Llangyfelach
- Caerwent †
- † Bishopston
- Llancarfan †
- † Llandaf

SCALE ⊢———⊣ 20 miles/32 km

† The main churches and early monasteries

Areas where churches had been dedicated to St David by about 1250

47

HISTORY GROUNDED

one of their followers had. Although none of these early churches can be seen today, archaeologists have found the remains of some of them in the foundations of later churches.

When we look at the names of towns and villages in Wales, it's obvious that some saints were much more popular than others. The most important saint in Wales was David, who is called Dewi in Welsh. There are lots of places in Wales called after him!

The yellow cross on a black background is the banner of the diocese of St Davids. It has become a flag to wave on patriotic occasions, like international football or rugby matches and the St David's Day celebrations.

There are churches dedicated to St David in Ireland, Brittany and England, as well as in Wales. This ancient and remarkable church is at Rhulen in the hills of Radnorshire. It was built about 1300. The churches of St David's time would have been much smaller than this.

HISTORY GROUNDED

The stories of two saints

St David

Lots of the stories about the Welsh saints are more stories than history. It's quite likely that many of them come from stories about the pagan gods and the places that were sacred to them. But in the case of St David – and St Patrick, the patron saint of Ireland too – we have more historical evidence. This makes us think that he was a real person.

We feel fairly sure that St David was born about 500, and that he died about 589, and he became famous for his extremely simple way of living. He preferred to eat vegetables and bread, at a time when meat was a very important food for everyone. He preferred to drink water when everyone else – including monks like St David – preferred to drink beer or mead. He was a very modest man who spent most of his time in prayer and meditation.

He became famous for his holy way of living, and people came to follow him, to try to copy his way of life. He may have founded a monastery at St David's, but there is nothing to be seen there from his time. But there are two things that still tell us something about him: one is the fact that he is called Dewi, not David, in Welsh, and this is an affectionate nickname, like Dai or Deio today. The other is the words from his last sermon, which have been kept for us in the story of his life which was written after his days.

David said, "Brothers and sisters, be happy, keep the faith, and do the little things that you have seen and heard with me."

St Non's Chapel, near St David's, Pembrokeshire. This is where St David was born, according to the legend.

HISTORY GROUNDED

Melangell

Melangell's story is a lot less certain There is no definite evidence for her, as there is for David, and legends are all we know about her. According to these legends, Melangell was the daughter of an Irish king. She ran away to Wales to escape a marriage that her father had arranged for her.

She went to live in a lonely place in the mountains of Powys, and lived there quietly for several years. But one day the prince of Powys, Brochfael Ysgithrog, met her when he was out hunting hares with his dogs. One of the hares ran towards Melangell, and hid by her feet. The dogs wouldn't touch the hare, and the huntsmen could do nothing with them. Brochfael was amazed, and decided Melangell must have supernatural powers – she must be a saint.

Brochfael gave Melangell the land around her home, and she set up a community there for women – nuns – to live a simple and holy life. According to the legends, that is where the church of Pennant Melangell stands today, and it is certain that this church was an important religious centre for centuries. The remains of a splendid shrine to Melangell can still be seen there today.

Pennant Melangell church in the remote hills of Montgomeryshire, Powys – this again is much bigger than the original church.

HISTORY GROUNDED

You can find evidence for these early churches across Wales. There are many churches dedicated to those saints who travelled by boat from one Celtic country to another to preach. And there are sites of monasteries and schools too.

One of the most important was the monastery founded by St Seiriol in Penmon, Anglesey (above). These buildings were built in the Middle Ages on a site which had been important to the early church. The saints are associated with healing springs in almost every parish in Wales, like St Cybi's Well at Llangybi, Eifionydd (below).

HISTORY GROUNDED

Some of the natural borders between the different areas of Wales. The Offa's Dyke Path is on the right.

HISTORY GROUNDED

OFFA'S DYKE AND OGHAM STONES

Incomers to Europe

As the Roman empire got weaker, more and more people came to live in the areas which had once been under a strong authority. It is very hard to follow the history of these years. It was a time of war and disorder, and nobody had the time to sit down and keep a record of what was happening, let alone write books about it. Many books were probably destroyed in these years too.

Offa's Dyke, near Bishop's Castle, Shropshire, where the present border between Wales and England crosses Offa's Dyke.

But when we look at maps of Europe today, we can see names which remind us of the people who came from the north and the east to push against Roman rule. There's France, named after the tribe of Franks, and the Welsh word for Germany, *yr Almaen*, comes from the Alemanni tribe. The French language has developed from Latin. But German is different, and belongs to a family of languages which includes Dutch and English.

The Welsh word for English people – *Saeson* – and their language – *Saesneg* – comes from Saxons, the name of a tribe which once lived on the northern edges of the Roman empire. Some of them came to live in eastern Britain. They made their homes there as the centuries went

HISTORY GROUNDED

on, and built dykes on the east of Wales to protect their lands. Offa's Dyke is the most famous of these, and is named after one of the Saxon kings. We often say in Welsh "going over Offa's Dyke" when we mean going to England.

Some very sad poems, *Canu Heledd,* describe the fighting between the Welsh and the Saxons in this time. Here is one very famous verse from one of these poems. A girl is visiting the home of her brother, Cynddylan, who has been killed in a battle:

Ystafell Cynddylan, ys tywyll heno,
The hall of Cynddylan is dark tonight,
Heb dân, heb wely.
No fire, no bed.
Wylaf wers, tawaf wedy.
I will weep for a while, then be silent.

Ogham writing on a stone in Llanwenog church, Ceredigion. There are words in Latin and Ogham on this stone. By comparing the two languages on stones like this one, experts managed to read Ogham for the first time for centuries.

In these words, someone from that time talks to us today.

Incomers to Wales

Between the 5C and the 10C, people from other countries came to live in Wales – and they left their mark on the country. Since Wales has a very long coastline, it's not surprising that many of these are near the sea.

Some people came over from Ireland, and the countryside in Pembrokeshire and Llŷn looks very like parts of Ireland. The high banks and the field patterns are the same. These people also put up

54

Maen Achwyfan Cross, Flintshire
Picture: an engraving by Moses Griffith in Thomas Pennant's book,
A Tour in Wales, 1810 edition.

Making Wales

About 615 the Welsh lost an important battle against the forces of Northumbria near Bangor-on-Dee, Wrexham. It is called the Battle of Chester. Monks from Wales were killed after the battle, and the tradition is that Maen Achwyfan was put up in Flintshire to remember that massacre. From this time on, we can begin to talk about Wales as a separate country apart from England. But the actual boundary often changes, and many people on the English side went on talking Welsh for centuries. "Cymru" is the word we use for the country, and "Cymry" for the people of the country, and it means "people who live in the same area". The name the Saxons – the early English people – gave us was "Welsh", which first meant "people who have been Romanised".

HISTORY GROUNDED

Archaeologists at work looking for the evidence of the past in Anglesey

The remains of Viking graves, Llanbedr-goch, Anglesey

HISTORY GROUNDED

gravestones, and the writing on these is in Irish – but it isn't writing we would recognise. This is the Ogham alphabet. Some people think this might have been a secret language. You could say one thing aloud, for everyone to hear, and then spell out something entirely different by moving your fingers against the side of your hand.

Other people came from a country further away, sailing over the sea from Scandinavia to Wales – and to lots of other countries in Europe as well. These people were called the Vikings, and they made their homes close to the sea. The English names of these places come from the Viking language, but apart from that they didn't leave much mark on the country.

It was a very different story on the east coast of Britain, which is closer to Scandinavia. A large part of the country we call England today was ruled by the Vikings for a long time. The great achievement of Alfred the Great (c. 848–899) was to defend his kingdom against the Vikings.

The coastline of Wales is dotted with Viking names, for example, Skokholm and Skomer (below). The ending '-ey' denotes an island (Anglesey/Bardsey); '-holm', a small island; and '-by' could refer to a house/farm (Womanby/Lamby in Cardiff).

HISTORY GROUNDED

Dinas Emrys in the middle of the mountains of Snowdonia

Y DDRAIG GOCH (THE RED DRAGON)

The Red Dragon has been the symbol of Wales for centuries, on shields and on flags. It's unusual because in most countries dragons are thought to be dangerous creatures. But, here in Wales, we have a dragon which protects us and inspires us! There is an old story about a castle being built in Dinas Emrys, near Beddgelert, Gwynedd. In a lake in a cave in the rock under the castle a red dragon was fighting against a white dragon. The red dragon won, and the white dragon flew away to England.

Kings used to be called "dragons" and they would carry banners with dragons on them. Perhaps you remember that the name of King Arthur's father was Uthr Pendragon – it means "the terrifying chief dragon"!

Bridge over the river Dyfi, Machynlleth

Boundaries that divide and join

When the first people settled and made their homes in Wales, the mountain ridges and the river valleys were the natural boundaries for the land they claimed. When these settlements began to join together to form small kingdoms, the highest mountains and the biggest rivers became the boundaries.

When we look at the Brecon Beacons today, it's easy to see how they divide the ancient kingdoms of Brycheiniog (Breconshire) and Morgannwg (Glamorgan). We can see too that the river Dyfi flows between the north and south regions of Wales. For centuries, the rivers Dee and Severn formed the boundary between Wales and England.

But there's always a pass – a gap between mountains, and a ford or a crossing place on a river. Enemies could use these weak spots to attack, and Welsh phrases like 'sefyll yn y bwlch' ('hold the pass') remind us vividly of those days when warriors fought on their boundaries.

HISTORY GROUNDED

Bwlch Maen Gwynedd on the Berwyn ridge

But countries can join together through a pass or a ford.

There is a pass through the Berwyn mountains which is marked by a standing stone called Bwlch Maen Gwynedd ('*the pass of the stone of Gwynedd*'). Nest, the daughter of Cadell, king of Powys, may have travelled this way to marry Merfyn Frych, the king of Gwynedd. Their son, Rhodri Mawr, became king of both Gwynedd and Powys in about 855.

Sometimes, a boundary is just a small mark on the ground that you can walk across. In some places it is only a little ditch running between two areas. There are two places called Ffos-y-ffin ('*boundary ditch*') in Wales and several called Ffinant ('*boundary stream*'). It doesn't matter how small it is – every boundary has a meaning because it shapes your cynefin. Boundaries can create a sense of belonging and identity, but they can divide us as well.

It's an old Welsh custom to use the names of rivers or mountains as personal names. The rugby player Berwyn Jones (1940–2007) is an example of that, as is Ann Clwyd, the MP for the Cynon Valley from 1984 to 2019.

HISTORY GROUNDED

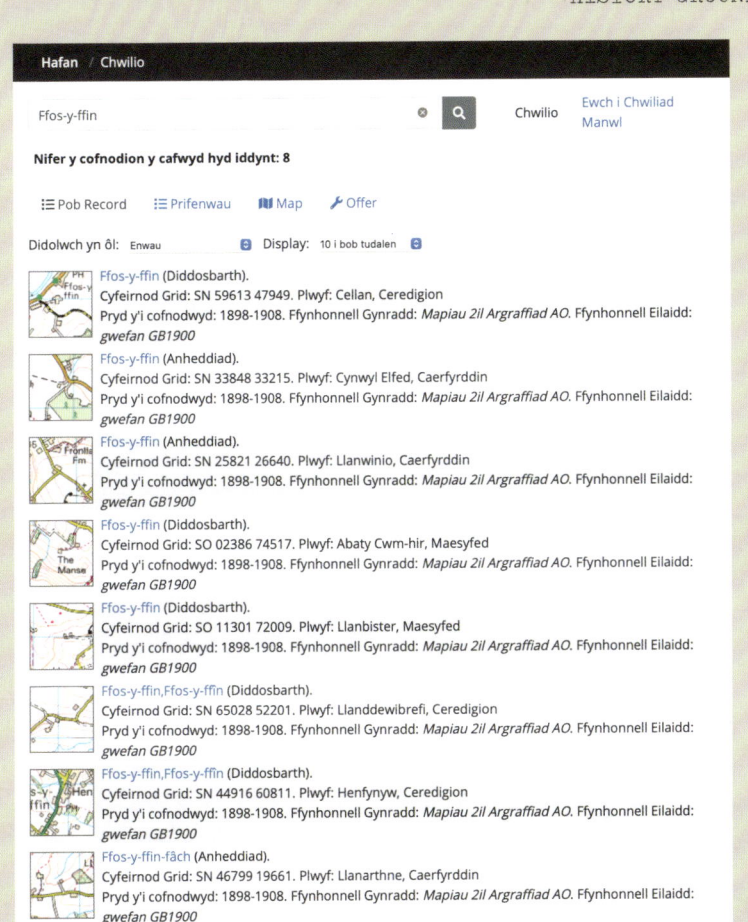

Hafan / Chwilio			
Ffos-y-ffin	🔍	Chwilio	Ewch i Chwiliad Manwl

Nifer y cofnodion y cafwyd hyd iddynt: 8

≣ Pob Record   ≣ Prifenwau   📖 Map   🔧 Offer

Didolwch yn ôl: Enwau   Display: 10 i bob tudalen

Ffos-y-ffin (Diddosbarth).
Cyfeirnod Grid: SN 59613 47949. Plwyf: Cellan, Ceredigion
Pryd y'i cofnodwyd: 1898-1908. Ffynhonnell Gynradd: *Mapiau 2il Argraffiad AO*. Ffynhonnell Eilaidd: gwefan GB1900

Ffos-y-ffin (Anheddiad).
Cyfeirnod Grid: SN 33848 33215. Plwyf: Cynwyl Elfed, Caerfyrddin
Pryd y'i cofnodwyd: 1898-1908. Ffynhonnell Gynradd: *Mapiau 2il Argraffiad AO*. Ffynhonnell Eilaidd: gwefan GB1900

Ffos-y-ffin (Anheddiad).
Cyfeirnod Grid: SN 25821 26640. Plwyf: Llanwinio, Caerfyrddin
Pryd y'i cofnodwyd: 1898-1908. Ffynhonnell Gynradd: *Mapiau 2il Argraffiad AO*. Ffynhonnell Eilaidd: gwefan GB1900

Ffos-y-ffin (Diddosbarth).
Cyfeirnod Grid: SO 02386 74517. Plwyf: Abaty Cwm-hir, Maesyfed
Pryd y'i cofnodwyd: 1898-1908. Ffynhonnell Gynradd: *Mapiau 2il Argraffiad AO*. Ffynhonnell Eilaidd: gwefan GB1900

Ffos-y-ffin (Diddosbarth).
Cyfeirnod Grid: SO 11301 72009. Plwyf: Llanbister, Maesyfed
Pryd y'i cofnodwyd: 1898-1908. Ffynhonnell Gynradd: *Mapiau 2il Argraffiad AO*. Ffynhonnell Eilaidd: gwefan GB1900

Ffos-y-ffin,Ffos-y-ffin (Diddosbarth).
Cyfeirnod Grid: SN 65028 52201. Plwyf: Llanddewibrefi, Ceredigion
Pryd y'i cofnodwyd: 1898-1908. Ffynhonnell Gynradd: *Mapiau 2il Argraffiad AO*. Ffynhonnell Eilaidd: gwefan GB1900

Ffos-y-ffin,Ffos-y-ffin (Diddosbarth).
Cyfeirnod Grid: SN 44916 60811. Plwyf: Henfynyw, Ceredigion
Pryd y'i cofnodwyd: 1898-1908. Ffynhonnell Gynradd: *Mapiau 2il Argraffiad AO*. Ffynhonnell Eilaidd: gwefan GB1900

Ffos-y-ffin-fâch (Anheddiad).
Cyfeirnod Grid: SN 46799 19661. Plwyf: Llanarthne, Caerfyrddin
Pryd y'i cofnodwyd: 1898-1908. Ffynhonnell Gynradd: *Mapiau 2il Argraffiad AO*. Ffynhonnell Eilaidd: gwefan GB1900

You can find out more about place names and the connections between places by going to the website of the Royal Commission on the Ancient and Historical Monuments in Wales (https://historicplacenames.rcahmw.gov.uk) and using the search window. There's often a story – or history – behind a name.

FFOS-Y-FFIN

A village in Ceredigion

Pulling someone's hair was a crime according the Laws of Hywel Dda. Like the laws of other countries in Europe in his time, these old Welsh laws encouraged people to settle their differences by paying compensation for a crime or a quarrel. Women's rights were also included in the Laws of Hywel Dda.

The Laws of Hywel Dda

After the fall of the Roman empire, there were years of endless fighting throughout Europe. Perhaps because of this, any king who could keep the peace in his kingdom was praised enormously. One of these was Hywel ap Cadell (880–948). To begin with, he was king only of south-west Wales, but he got the other kings of Wales to accept his leadership. He earned praise for sorting out the different laws and customs which existed in Wales at that time. King Alfred did the same in his kingdom, as did the Emperor Charlemagne in his empire, which included France and Germany. The lawbooks of Ireland are very like these too.

But maybe all these laws don't show us what life was like then, but describe what it should have been like. All the same, for centuries the Laws of Hywel Dda were the basis for whatever law and order there was in Wales. From now on, we will depend on information from these laws when we GUESS how people lived in Wales.

HISTORY GROUNDED

Hywel Dda memorial gardens in Whitland

A mystery in a church

Who is this little warrior?

We have to make a lot of guesses when we try to find out about the past. This stone is in Eglwysilan church, on the mountain between Pontypridd and Caerphilly in Glamorgan. But nobody knows anything about it, except that it is very old, and was found buried in the graveyard in 1904. Some people think it shows a warrior of the time of Hywel Dda, others that it could have been made 200 years later. But there are no Christian symbols on the stone, and this little warrior could belong to the time before Christianity.

The carving of a warrior in Eglwysilan church, near Caerphilly

63

HISTORY GROUNDED

| 1000 | 1100 | 1200 | 1300 |

Motte-and-bailey 1070   **Welsh castle** 1170   **Glyndŵr** 1404

| 1000 | 1100 | 1200 | 1300 |

Dates

Part 2: Timeline

Questions

- What types of castles were first built by the Normans?
- How did the princes of Wales live?

64

HISTORY GROUNDED

| 1500 | 1600 | 1700 | 1800 |

Welsh Bible 1588 **Mansions of the gentry c.1650** **Slavery c.1750**

- Why is Glyndŵr so important to Welsh people?
- Why was translating the Bible into Welsh so vital?
- How comfortable were the houses of the well-off?
- What did Wales have to do with the slave trade?

HISTORY GROUNDED

The kingdoms of Wales in about 1000

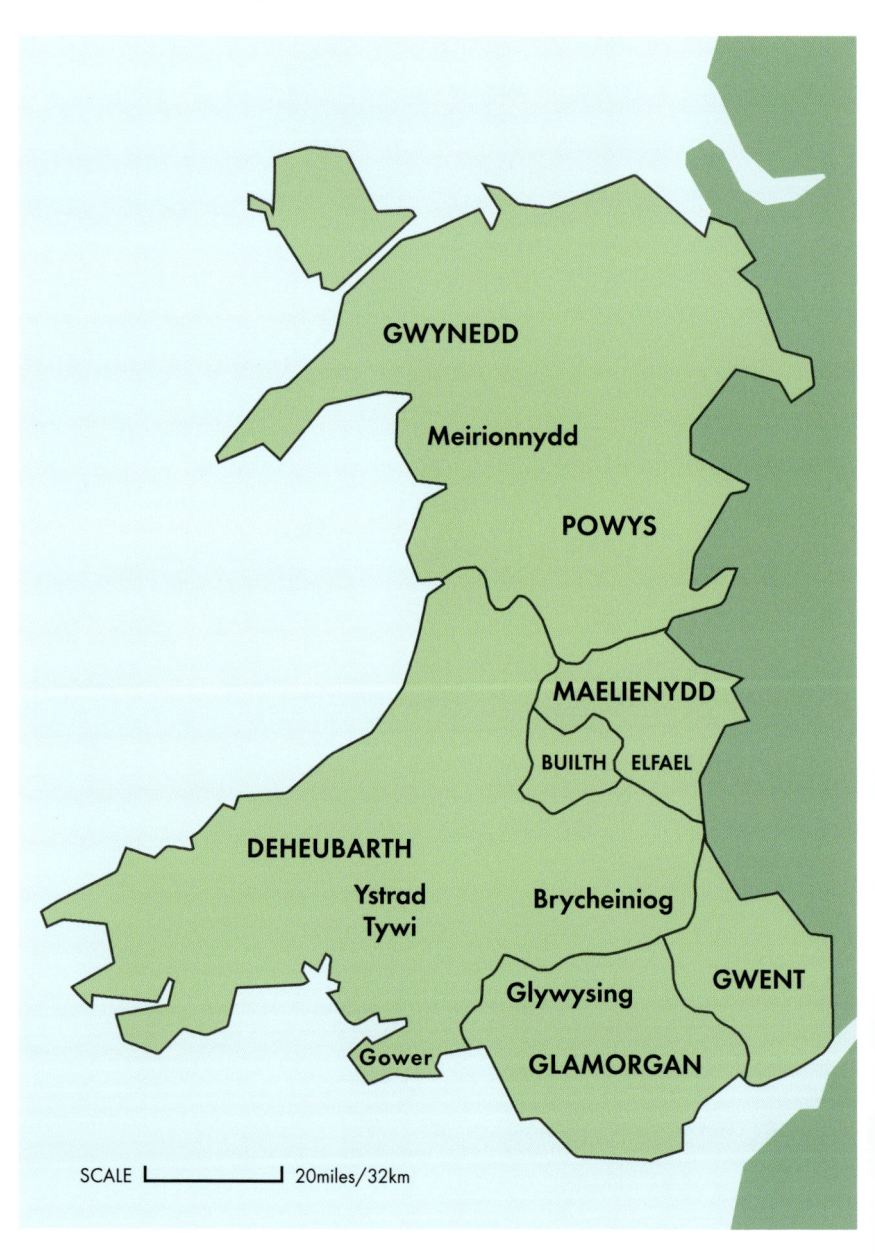

GWYNEDD

Meirionnydd

POWYS

MAELIENYDD

BUILTH ELFAEL

DEHEUBARTH

Ystrad Tywi

Brycheiniog

Glywysing

GWENT

Gower

GLAMORGAN

SCALE 20 miles / 32 km

HISTORY GROUNDED

Dividing and joining the kingdoms of Wales

By about AD 1000 five large kingdoms had developed in Wales: Gwynedd, Powys, Deheubarth, Gwent and Morgannwg. The size of each kingdom varied a lot. Its boundaries depended on how good a ruler was in keeping his own land safe – and in taking land from the other rulers around him. On top of that, when a king died, the custom in Wales was to divide his land between his sons. But you can see the names of these old kingdoms in Wales today

There were signs though that all these kingdoms could become one. One strong leader called Gruffudd ap Llywelyn managed to bring them all together between 1057 and 1063.

A statue in the mountains of Snowdonia to celebrate the long struggle of the Welsh to keep their land

HISTORY GROUNDED

White Castle in Monmouthshire – one of the Norman castles in east Wales

The Normans in Wales

One of the names for the Vikings was Northmen, "the men from the north". When some of them made their homes in the north-west of France, that area became known as "Normandy". From 1066, the Normans, the people of Normandy, began to play an important part in the history of the British Isles. When the king of England had died without an heir, the Duke of Normandy – William the Conqueror – came over with a big army and won the battle of Hastings in south-east England. He was crowned king on Christmas Day 1066.

The Normans then conquered all of England over the next year, and started to attack Wales at the same time. But it took over 200 years for them to conquer Wales. They found it hard to conquer Ireland and didn't succeed in conquering Scotland at all.

So, the centuries after 1066 were years of endless wars. Sometimes the Normans would attack, but there was fighting between the Normans too, and between the Welsh themselves, and sometimes between the Welsh and the Normans together against other Welsh and Normans. These were terribly cruel years in Wales.

HISTORY GROUNDED

The first castles in Wales and the Norman invasions about 1100

- Deganwy
- Rhos
- Rhuddlan
- Tegeingl
- **EARL OF CHESTER**
- Maelor
- Edeirnion
- Cynllaith
- **EARL OF SHREWSBURY**
- Shrewsbury
- Montgomery
- Arwystli
- Kerry
- **EARL MORTIMER**
- Wigmor
- New Radnor
- **EARL OF HEREFORD**
- Cardigan
- Builth
- Hereford
- Brecon
- Abergavenny
- Monmouth
- Pembroke
- Gower
- Chepstow
- Cardiff

SCALE 20miles/32km

HISTORY GROUNDED

The princes of Wales

There have been lots of princes – and princesses too – in Wales, and there are stories about them in every part of the country. But after 200 years the princes of Gwynedd had succeeded in bringing most of Wales into one kingdom. One of the princes of Gwynedd is called "Llywelyn Fawr – the Great" because he did so much to make this happen. His grandson Llywelyn ap Gruffudd has a different title. He is "Llywelyn Ein Llyw Olaf – Our Last Prince" because he was the last independent prince of Wales. He was killed near Cilmeri, Builth, in 1282 and the Normans took his only child, Princess Gwenllian, to a nunnery in the east of England, and she died there. She never saw Wales again. It wasn't long afterwards that Edward I, the king of England, conquered all of Wales.

A memorial to Lord Rhys, one of the princes of Deheubarth, in Cardigan (above) and a memorial to Llywelyn Fawr in Conwy

HISTORY GROUNDED

A memorial to Gwenllian who led a Welsh army against the Normans at Cydweli in 1136, and the stone marking Llywelyn ap Gruffudd's death at Cilmeri. These memorials were all put up in the 20C.

In 1993 some Welsh people put up this memorial stone at Sempringham Abbey in Lincolnshire, in the east of England. In that abbey princess Gwenllian lived out her whole life as a nun. How much did she know about her own history, I wonder? Although all these are modern memorials, they are very like the stones raised over graves in the Early Times. They show too how much interest people take in Welsh history today – and in the part women have played in that history.

HISTORY GROUNDED

Norman castles

The Normans have left their mark on every part of Wales. They were the first to build some of the most famous buildings in our country – the castles. Norman kings built strong castles and they expected everyone who owned land to build a castle to defend it.

The simplest castle, and the easiest one to build was a motte-and-bailey castle. The 'bailey' is the flat ground below the mound of earth called a 'motte'. They would dig a ditch around the bailey, and the earth from that would make the motte. Then they cut down trees to make a fence around the ditch and to build a tower on the motte. All you needed was a saw – and spadework.

The people living in the areas the Normans took over were forced to build the castles. Then they had to work for their conquerors and give them some of the crops from their fields. The first wooden castles were sometimes rebuilt in stone, but that didn't always happen. There are 500 motte-and-bailey castles in Wales. Often it is only the mound of earth that shows there was a castle there once – about 900 years ago.

One of the first stone castles in Wales was the central tower of Chepstow castle, which was built in 1070. The Welsh learnt to build castles too, like Castell Dolbadarn and Castell Dinefwr.

The remains of a big Norman motte at Painscastle, Radnorshire (left), and a motte-and-bailey castle which was later made stronger by having a stone tower built on the motte: Wiston castle, Pembrokeshire (right)

HISTORY GROUNDED

The picture above shows how the motte-and-bailey castle in Cardiff might have looked in the 12C. Below is a picture of the castle today, with its stone tower. A high fence, of tree trunks, would be built to defend the motte and bailey. The stables, the workshops, the kitchens and so on would be in the bailey. You could get all the building materials you needed locally, and these first wooden castles could be built in about ten days. It would probably be the local people who had just been conquered who would have been forced to build these castles.

The main weapon of the Welsh when they attacked the early motte-and-bailey castles was fire. Since the buildings were mostly made of wood, setting fire to these castles was a very good way of getting rid of the enemy. When the Normans began to build stone walls and towers, it was more difficult to attack them – but not impossible.

An exciting story is told about Cardiff castle. Gerald of Wales tells us that one night in 1158, the prince of Senghennydd, Ifor ap Meurig ("Ifor Bach") and his people got into the castle. William Fitz Robert, the Norman lord of Cardiff, had taken some land from Ifor. Ifor kidnapped the lord, his wife and their son, and kept them prisoners in the hills until the Norman gave the land back to Ifor!

HISTORY GROUNDED

The Normans started to build their first stone castles in Wales in 1067 – Chepstow castle on a cliff on the Welsh side of the river Wye.

From about 1200 on, the Normans in England began to lose much of their land in France. Although they still spoke French, they began to call themselves English. In Wales, Welsh was the main language. At this time there were lots of wars between the king in London and the French. This was very useful to the Welsh because they could take advantage of the king's 'absence' on some campaign in France to win back their own land.

After Llywelyn Ein Llyw Olaf was killed, Edward I took his kingdom. He built a number of huge, strong castles to make sure he kept his hold on Gwynedd. They are still there now, and today you can go in

Dolbadarn Castle in the mountains of Gwynedd

Carreg Cennen castle on the rock overlooking the fields of the Tywi Valley

and out of them without being afraid. You can walk around them, and look out from their towers across the countryside without thinking about keeping yourself safe in war. But the fact that there are so many of these castles and the sheer size of ones like Harlech, Rhuddlan and Caernarfon still show us today how frightened the English kings were of war in Wales.

Caerphilly castle is the biggest castle in Wales – and one of the biggest in Europe. It was built by Earl Gilbert de Clare, who was afraid of Llywelyn ap Gruffudd's power over the Welsh of Glamorgan.

For centuries, the Welsh had to defend themselves against attacks from their enemies. Against the Normans their strongest weapon was the longbow. This was developed in Glamorgan and Gwent – where the Normans attacked first. The long bow changed the way battles were fought from then on. A Welsh longbowman could wound a soldier in armour by shooting an arrow into him from 150 metres away. And an arrowhead could go through a wooden door 10cm thick in a castle doorway.

HISTORY GROUNDED

Wales 1282–1295

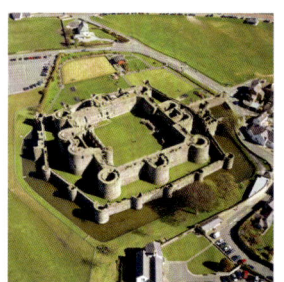

- Courts/castles of the Welsh princes
- Castles of Edward I
- Centres of government

Locations shown on map:
- Flint
- Rhuddlan
- Conwy
- Beaumaris
- Llys Aberffraw
- Llys Rhosyr
- Llys Abergwyngregyn
- Hawarden
- Chester
- Ruthin
- Caernarfon
- Dinas Brân
- Criccieth
- Chirk
- Harlech
- Llys Mathrafal
- Shrewsbury
- Dolforwyn
- Montgomery
- Aberystwyth
- Ludlow
- Builth
- Cardigan
- Brecon
- Hereford
- Dinefwr
- Carmarthen
- Abergavenny
- Haverfordwest
- St Clears
- Kidwelly
- Pembroke
- Swansea
- Cardiff

SCALE 20 miles/32km

Rhuddlan, Caernarfon and Beaumaris castles

76

A prince and a princess

Gruffudd ap Cynan (c. 1055-1137)

We know more about Gruffudd ap Cynan than any other prince of Wales. The story of his life was written down, and some of the stories in it read as if Gruffudd himself had told them. He says, for example, that he was really lazy when he was a boy, and tried to dodge doing his schoolwork – which was learning to fight. That was the main thing any young man from a noble family had to learn in the Middle Ages, and for a long time after that. But one day, as he was watching the *cawl* boiling in the cauldron, he saw that there was one piece of meat which kept bobbing up to the top. He decided he was going to be like that piece of meat – he would get to the top, whatever happened.

The site of one of Gruffudd's battles after he came back from Ireland: Bron-yr-erw on the side of Bwlch Mawr mountain between Arfon and Eifionydd.

Three of Gruffudd ap Cynan's biggest enemies were Hugh the Fat, lord of Chester; Roger, lord of Shrewsbury, and Hugh's cousin, Robert of Rhuddlan, whose castle was on this motte beside the river Clwyd.

He didn't have a quiet life and he did have to work hard to get to the top. He was brought up in Ireland, and then he had to fight some of his own family to get to rule Gwynedd. When he won the battle of Mynydd Carn in 1081, he had safe hold of Gwynedd. But then he was captured by the Normans, who had just taken over Chester. Gruffudd spent at least twelve years as a prisoner in Chester before he managed to escape in 1094, and take possession of Gwynedd a second time. The Normans came with an army to try and drive him out, but he beat them in a battle on the shores of the Menai Strait – with the help of the Vikings. From then on he had some quite peaceful years, and his son Owain inherited a united kingdom without any fighting.

HISTORY GROUNDED

Nest ferch Rhys ap Tewdwr
(about 1085–sometime after 1136)

There is not much about women or girls in the chronicles that tell us the history of the Middle Ages. These were written by men, and men were the important ones. Sometimes we don't even know the name of a prince's mother, and nobody would bother to note the date a woman died. This is true of Princess Nest – nobody knows when she died. But, because of what happened to her, we know more about her than most of the princesses of this time. She didn't manage to overcome her difficulties as Gruffudd ap Cynan did, and she had no control over her own life.

Pembroke castle

Nest was the daughter of Rhys ap Tewdwr, the last independent prince of Deheubarth. Her father was killed in a battle against the Normans in 1093. The Normans captured Nest's two brothers and killed them. Nest was taken as a privileged prisoner to the court of King William Rufus. While she was there, she had a child with Henry, the king's brother. The king then married Nest off to one of his friends, Gerald of Windsor. The king had chosen Gerald to look after Pembroke for him, and Nest went to live there with her husband in 1105. She and Gerald had at least five children, but in 1109 Nest was kidnapped by her cousin, Owain ap Cadwgan of Powys. In the end Owain had to give Nest back to her husband.

When Gerald died, Nest's sons arranged for her to marry Stephen, the constable of Cardigan castle, and she may have married a fifth husband too. But it doesn't seem that she ever had much of a say in the decisions that were made about her.

HISTORY GROUNDED

In 1188 a man called Gerald travelled through Wales to try to get soldiers to fight against the Muslims in Jerusalem. He was Princess Nest's grandson, and was related to many Welsh princes and Norman lords.

He thought of himself as a Norman, although we call him Gerald of Wales, and wrote a description of his journey through Wales, partly to help the Normans to overcome the Welsh. But he gives us fascinating details about how Welsh people lived – and cleaned their teeth! On his travels he collected all sorts of stories which no one else had

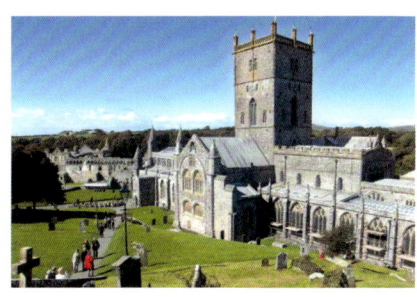

St David's Cathedral

recorded. We learn too how difficult it was to travel in some parts of Wales, especially when you had to cross rivers. This is the first description of travelling in Wales, which makes it really valuable.

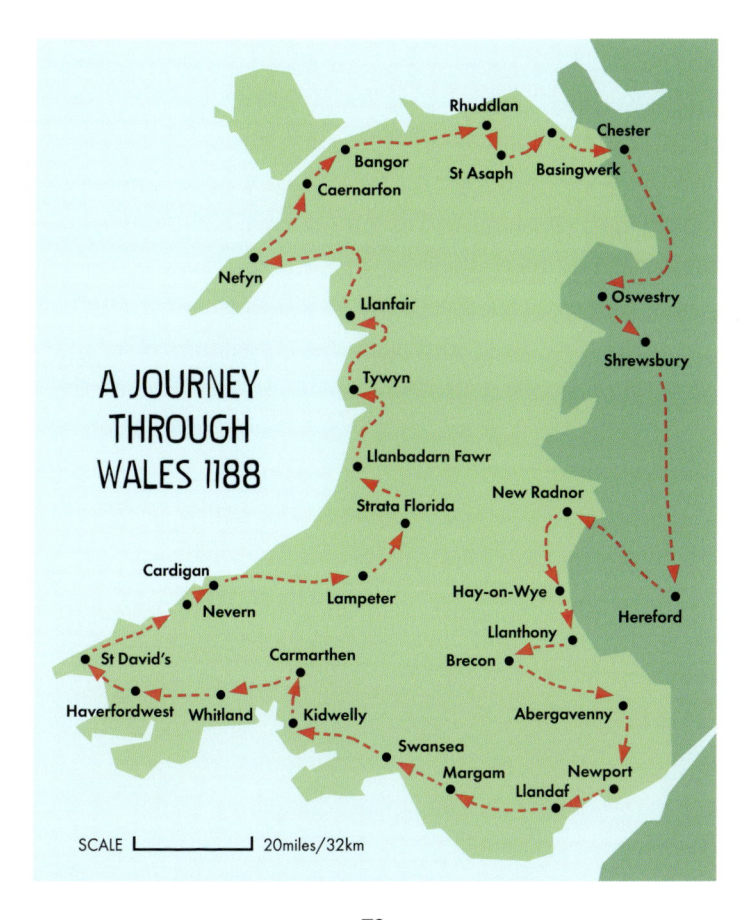

A JOURNEY THROUGH WALES 1188

SCALE 20miles/32km

HISTORY GROUNDED

Llys Rhosyr has been recreated at St Fagan's National Museum of History. Archaeological evidence from the site in Anglesey was used as a basis for the work and specialists on the history, architecture and literature of Wales also helped the Museum with the design.

Living like a prince

So, every part of Wales had its own royal family, and there are stories and legends about every family, from Anglesey to Gwent. There are stories about brave princesses, like Gwenllian of Deheubarth, about daring princes, like Ifor Bach of Senghennydd, about princes who were poets too, like Hywel ab Owain Gwynedd. But don't expect to know much about anyone except princes in this period. Only stories about important men were written down. There were sure to have been lots of interesting stories about ordinary people too – but in those days no-one thought they were worth writing down.

Don't think either that the princes of Wales lived in big castles, or wore suits of armour and colourful clothes. The courts of these princes were just wooden buildings to begin with, and they would have lots of these across their kingdoms. They would travel from one to another during the year, and there were lots of practical reasons for doing this.

First of all, every prince was expected to keep law and order in his kingdom. He had to hold courts of law to deal with criminals, and sort out family quarrels. The people of each area paid a rent of food and work to their ruler, and the work had to be checked – and the food eaten too! There were no tins or freezers then. And finally, every building had to be cleaned. Every prince travelled with a crowd of people, and in every age a lot of people leave a lot of mess. Also – people didn't wash themselves or their clothes very often, and only important people had toilets!

HISTORY GROUNDED

But there were toilets in the castles. A small room would be built out of the highest part of the outside wall of the castle, so that everything from the toilet would fall into the moat. You can see a row of these on the walls of Conwy – and you don't have to pay to go into the castle.

81

Valle Crucis Abbey as it looks today (above) and a drawing (below) to show how Tintern Abbey might have looked in the Middle Ages

Churches and monasteries

Castles aren't the only Norman buildings to be seen in Wales. The oldest parts of many Welsh churches belong to this time too. The church would be the biggest building in a village, and the centre of everything that went on there too. The tower would shelter people in wartime, and the church holidays and celebrations gave people a chance to have fun together. Religion was very important to people at this time, and people believed that they could please God by giving him gifts. So, rich people would give lots of land to the church. The people who lived there would pay their rents to the church then, not to the local lord.

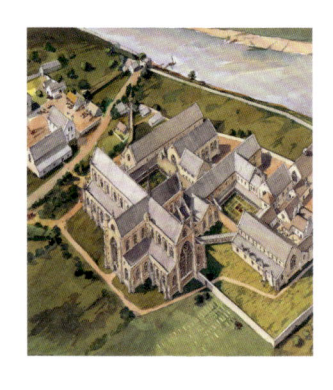

Many people at this time chose to give their lives to God. They would spend every day of their lives serving him by praying or by doing other work in God's name, like caring for the poor and the ill, or copying out religious books. These men are called monks, and women are called nuns. The ruins of the places where they lived, monasteries like Tintern, Valle Crucis and Strata Florida show us how important religion was at that time, and how rich the churches were.

Abbeys and Monasteries

Map of Wales showing:

- **Bangor diocese**: Aberconwy
- **St Asaph's diocese**: Basingwerk, Valle Crucis, Strata Marcella
- **St David's diocese**: Cymer, Llanllugan, Strata Florida, Cwm-hir, Llanllŷr, Whitland
- **Llandaf diocese**: Llanthony, Tintern, Neath, Llantarnam, Margam

SCALE: 20 miles / 32 km

- ○ Cistercian abbeys
- † Benedictine abbeys
- • Other monasteries and priories

HISTORY GROUNDED

The priory of Llanddewi Nant Hodni ("Llanthony") in a "remote" place in the mountains, but it was an important centre for farming, wool and trade.

Even the shapes of fields can tell us a lot about old ways of farming. In the Middle Ages farmers would plough long, thin strips of land. The long fields in Uwchmynydd, near Aberdaron, show this clearly. It's worth looking at Google Earth: https://about.google/brand-resource-center/products-and-services/geo-guidelines/

HISTORY GROUNDED

An image of a traditional *hendref* in Thomas Pennant's *Tours in Wales*

Welsh farmers

Although you can grow crops like barley and rye in Wales, especially in areas like Anglesey and the Vale of Glamorgan, the weather and the type of soil meant that most farmers in Wales kept animals. They would take them to graze on the hills in the summer, and would build a house for themselves there – the *hafod*, "the summer place". But in the autumn they would bring their herds back to the old home – the *hendref*. You see these words in many Welsh place names today.

Over the centuries, Welsh farmers had had to pay rent for their land to whoever owned it, and that rent would be paid in food, because money wasn't used much. If there was a poor summer, and the crops failed, it would be difficult, if not impossible, to pay the rent. Thousands and thousands of Welsh people in the past must have died of starvation, or of the kinds of illnesses it is hard to get better from if you are starving. Some lords were willing for the farmers not to pay rent in times of famine. But some insisted on being paid, and sometimes a rebellion would start against a cruel lord.

Many of the Welsh people still thought of the English as their enemies too. They felt that their laws were unfair and harsher than the laws of Hywel Dda. The laws of Hywel Dda were still being used in some areas.

HISTORY GROUNDED

The world of the gentry and the poets

Before 1282 the poets of the princes praised them for being brave fighters. They would praise them too for being generous and giving wine and gold and horses to the poets. Poets would travel from court to court, and compete for prizes. Lord Rhys, one of the princes of Deheubarth, held a famous eisteddfod in his castle in Cardigan in 1176. A poet from north Wales won the chair for poetry, and a harpist from the south the chair for music. A chair is still the biggest prize in the National Eisteddfod today – although there have been lots of changes in the world and in eisteddfodau over the centuries!

After 1282, when there were no more princes in Wales, the poets went on visiting the homes of the gentry – the rich landowners. They would tell of the Mab Darogan, the prince who would lead the Welsh to victory against the English, as Arthur had done in the Welsh legends. Some thought Glyndŵr was the Mab Darogan. Then, in 1485, other people were certain that Henry Tudor was the leader they had been waiting for so long.

When they praised the gentry, the poets would often praise their homes. Because of this, there are detailed descriptions in the poetry that bring these homes to life, the families there and how they enjoyed themselves. There is only a mound of earth to be seen today in Sycharth, the home of Owain Glyndŵr – but the poet Iolo Goch describes it for us beautifully.

Cardigan bridge and castle

HISTORY GROUNDED

Poets and gentry enjoying life

Dafydd ap Gwilym is one of the greatest of Welsh poets, and in one of his poems he describes how he would enjoy a day with Ifor ap Llywelyn, the lord of Bassaleg, near Newport, Here is part of it:

Mi a gaf, o fyddaf byw
I will have, if I live,
Hela â chŵn, nid haelach ior,
Hunting with dogs – such a generous lord!,
Ac yfed gydag Ifor,
And drinking with Ifor,
A saethu rhygeirw sythynt,
And shooting strong, swift deer,
A bwrw gweilch i wybr a gwynt,
And sending hawks into the sky and the wind,
A cherddau tafodau teg,
And singing with sweet voices,
A solas ym Masaleg.
And comfort in Bassaleg.

A plaque to mark Dafydd ap Gwilym's birthplace.

A mound of earth is all that remains of Glyndŵr's court at Sycharth (right). But at Tretower, Powys, you can see what a feast might have looked like in the hall of a wealthy nobleman in the 1460s.

HISTORY GROUNDED

Battles were bloody and cruel in the Middle Ages too.

Rebels

By 1400 the English had made themselves at home in Wales. They'd built their castles, imported their monks and their church organisation, and forced their laws and customs on the people of Wales. They had also married into the families of the old princes, and the Welsh were beginning to follow new ways.

Fighting was still the focus of the lords' lives, and it was a time of constant war and rebellion. The church tried to turn this towards 'religious' war against the Moors in Spain or the Cathars in France. The most famous of these 'religious' wars are the Crusades, an unsuccessful attempt to win back the holy city of Jerusalem from the Muslims.

The king had the right to call on help from his lords when he went to war, and every lord had the right to call on help from his tenants – the knights who had been given a piece of land by him. The English would leave Wales when they went to war overseas, and this was the time when a rebellion was likely to start. There was a series of them between 1282 and 1400. Every single one failed, but the last rebellion is very important in Welsh history.

Owain Glyndŵr (1359–about 1415)

On 16 September 1400, Owain Glyndŵr, one of the most important lords in north Wales, decided to go to war against another of the local lords. Rebellion began to spread like wildfire throughout Wales. Glyndŵr was descended from the princes of Gwynedd and Powys, he was well respected and an experienced soldier. More importantly, he had new ideas, energy and the backing to make his ideas happen.

He succeeded in capturing or destroying the Norman castles. But while he was destroying castles in Wales, he was also building connections with the princes and kings of Europe, and with the Pope, the head of the church. His letters to them set out his ideas: a Wales independent from the king of England, with two universities and the right to appoint Welshmen to lead the church. He probably sent a letter to the king of France from the parliament he held in the village of Pennal, near Machynlleth, in 1406.

But Glyndŵr's time was short. He succeeded when the king of England, Henry IV, was fighting with his own people. When Henry had won that war, he turned his attention to his problem in Wales.

Glyndŵr's banner during celebrations in Corwen

Memorials to Owain Glyndŵr in the town of Corwen — the area where his revolt began (below) — and in Machynlleth, where the first Welsh parliament was held (middle)

HISTORY GROUNDED

The church at Pennal, where Owain Glyndŵr held one of his parliaments. The picture on the right is based on the image of Glyndŵr on his Great Seal which he would have used in parliament.

He sent his eldest son, one of the best soldiers of the time, with all the English army, against Glyndŵr. It took four years, but in the end the man who had once ruled all Wales only had Harlech castle left.

But Glyndŵr managed to escape from Harlech, and no one knows to this day where or when he died. There is nothing to be seen today of his splendid house at Sycharth. The castles he captured were taken back by the English. The building in Machynlleth called "Glyndŵr's Parliament House" was built after his time. Glyndŵr's ideas were only a dream, after all, but lots of people still celebrate Glyndŵr's Day on 16 September every year. And you can visit Pennal church, where Glyndŵr signed one of his letters to the king of France, and see the small exhibition about him there.

Cannon balls used in the attack on Harlech castle when the English were besieging it

HISTORY GROUNDED

Glyndŵr burnt many of the English castles and their towns too. He targeted these because English shopkeepers and craftspeople lived in the towns. These English people had lots of privileges that weren't given to the Welsh who lived outside the town walls. They had the right to hold markets, for example, and it was the officials of the market who set the prices on the produce of the farms.

Glyndŵr and his army attacked Caernarfon and burnt the town several times (top). He took Harlech castle (bottom) in 1404 and made it his headquarters and a safe home for his family.

Gwerful Mechain (c. 1460-1500)

During these centuries unmarried girls were thought to be the property of their fathers. A girl's father decided whom his daughter would marry, and he would give his daughter to her husband in the wedding ceremony. That still happens in lots of weddings today, and many people still think it is pretty tradition. But for a long time it showed clearly how little power any girl had, no matter how wealthy she was.

And getting married was the only choice a girl had, unless she wanted to give her life to God and become a nun. The story of Nest has shown us what can happen even to a princess. But, despite everything, sometimes a remarkable woman will succeed in overcoming every obstacle, and to make something of her own life. One such woman was Gwerful Mechain.

The craft of poetry is very important in Wales, and one of the most important ceremonies in the Eisteddfod today is crowning or chairing the bard. The bard who wins the chair has had to write poetry in the strict metres.

Mererid Hopwood – the first woman to win the Chair at a National Eisteddfod. She achieved this at Denbigh in 2001.

Every single line has to follow complicated patterns that knit the sounds together. These patterns are ancient and complex. Poets had a high status in the laws of Hywel Dda, and before that too. But every single poet we know about from this time is a man – except for Gwerful Mechain. She succeeded in mastering the strict metres, to compose poems about lots of different things, and to challenge some of the best poets of her day. We know very little about

The Virgin Mary on her throne, from an old Welsh manuscript (Llanbeblig Book of Hours)

her. It is only her poetry which proves to us that she ever lived. I wonder how many other brilliant women lived and died without having an opportunity to show what they could do?

HISTORY GROUNDED

Plas Penmynydd, Anglesey – the original home of the Tudors

MANSIONS
A Welsh King of England

Before Gwerful Mechain died, she would have seen a Welsh dream come true – a Welshman crowned king of England. In 1485 Henry VII won the English crown by beating his cousin Richard III in battle at Bosworth. Henry didn't have much right to the crown. His grandfather, Owain Tudur, had married Queen Catherine, the widow of Henry V who had beaten Glyndŵr. But the English royal family had been fighting amongst themselves for years, and by 1480 Henry Tudor was the hope of one group of the family, the Lancastrians.

Henry VII

Henry was born in Pembroke castle, and spent his childhood in Rhaglan castle. The two castles are still standing. Rhaglan castle is a good example of a castle from the Middle Ages which is starting to

HISTORY GROUNDED

All across Wales, the mansions and houses of the Tudor gentry show how rich and how ambitious they were.

Gwydir, near Llanrwst

Llancaeach Fawr, near Caerphilly

Bodysgallen, near Llandudno

Aberglasney, near Llandeilo

change into a comfortable mansion to live in, instead of being only a safe place in wartime. But Henry's family knew that his life was in danger, because the other part of the royal family, the Yorkists, were his enemies. So Henry had to live in France for years.

By 1485, Richard III, from the York family, was king of England, but Henry Tudor decided to try to take the crown. He landed in Dale, on the coast of Pembrokeshire, with a small army. He went on through Wales, picking up supporters on the way. Richard came with his army to meet him at Bosworth, near Leicester. Richard was killed in the battle, and Henry was crowned Henry VII.

This is the last time anyone won the crown of England in battle. Although Henry's claim to the throne was so poor, he managed to overcome everyone else, and to make sure that his son, Henry VIII, became king after him. For centuries there had been wars between the king and his lords, and between those lords amongst themselves, but these wars ended in Tudor times. From then on castles began to lose their importance and rich people began to build comfortable mansions, and not buildings to keep them safe in wartime.

Luxury living in Plas Mawr, Conwy

HISTORY GROUNDED

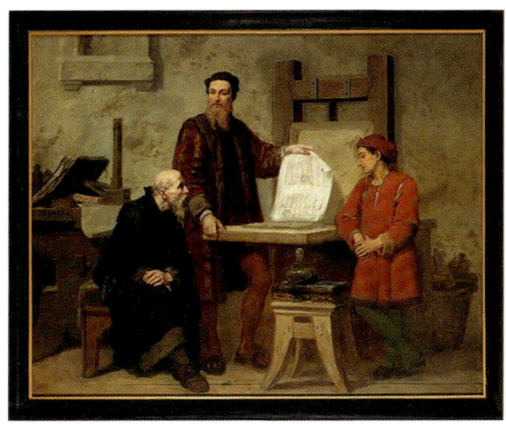

Johann Gutenberg from Germany invented the printing press, and changed the book publishing world

A time of peace is good for trade to grow too, and houses like Plas Mawr in Conwy show how wealthy Welsh businessmen were in towns in Wales.

A Religious Revolution

But other changes were happening during the time of Henry VII. In 1492 an adventurer called Christopher Columbus sailed to the west, in the hope of reaching India. But he reached the American continent – a new world to the people of Europe. There was a lot of gold and silver there, and for years Spanish ships carried the treasures of America back to Europe. Bit by bit, gold and silver lost their value, because there was now so much of them in Europe.

Earlier that century, Johann Gutenberg from Germany invented an easy way of printing books. Until then, the only way to get a new copy of a book was for someone to copy it out by hand. As time went by, it became possible for ordinary people to buy books.

For centuries, the authority of the Catholic Church, and of the Pope as the head of the Church, had been really strong. Every country in Europe belonged to the Catholic Church. The priests of the Church crowned kings in God's name. They christened every child, married every man and woman, and held the ceremonies when someone died. On the whole, only priests and monks could write. And it they who kept all the records and wrote every important document.

The Catholic Church was very rich too, because people gave it gifts in order to please God. Lords would give it land and pay the priests for prayers. On top of that, everybody had to give 10% of their income to the Church every year. As money began to lose its value, some kings started to look enviously at the Church's wealth.

Other changes were happening too. People began to criticise the Catholic Church for its wealth and its traditions, asking how far these were

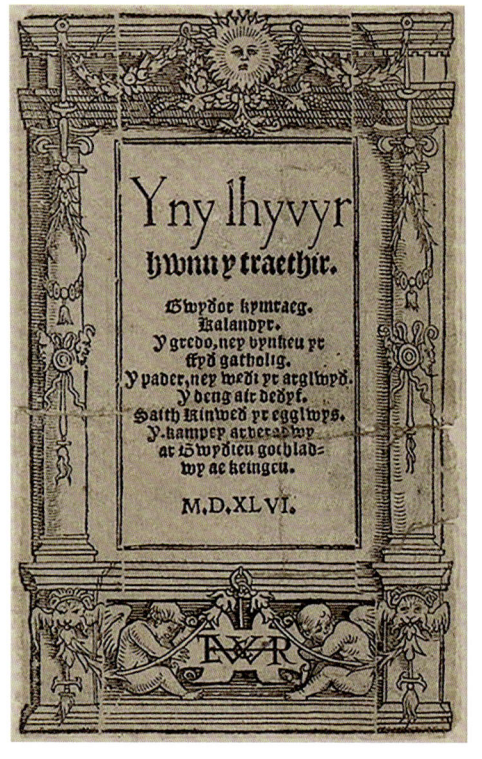

The title page of *Yny lhyvyr hwnn* (1546) – the first book to be published in Welsh

based on the teaching of the Bible. Men like Martin Luther and John Calvin had strong arguments against the Catholic Church, and these were becoming more and more popular in the time of Henry VIII. And when the Pope refused to allow Henry VIII to divorce his wife Catherine, Henry decided to do away with the authority of the Pope over his kingdom. Then he announced that he himself was the head of the church in England and Wales.

This was a real revolution – the king's officials went to every monastery and nunnery, closed them and took all their wealth. The treasures of gold, silver and jewels were taken from the cathedrals and the parish churches too. The king got much richer, and so did his lords and their followers.

Wales – a part of England

This revolution was a tragedy for many people. The churches and the monasteries were a very important part of their lives. The church's ceremonies, its colourful windows and walls, brought beauty and comfort to them. A lot of Welsh people were sad to lose their "Hen Fam" – their "Old Mother" – the Catholic Church. Wales has a long coastline and for thousands of years ships have been travelling between Welsh ports and those of France and Spain – two countries that had stayed faithful to the Catholic Church. The king and his counsellors were afraid that enemies from those countries might attack England from Wales – as Henry VII had done.

So, Henry VIII decided to get a stronger grip on Wales, by passing laws to make Wales a part of England. Wales was divided into counties, with officials to look after these for the king. Only the laws of England were to be kept, and Welsh people had to forget about the Laws of Hywel Dda. English, not Welsh, was to be the official language of Wales from then on.

Perhaps today it is only the names of some counties that show that these enormous changes happened at all. Perhaps most people in Wales didn't think much about them, except for the religious changes

> ...and also that from henceforth no Person or Persons that use the Welch Speech or Language, shall have or enjoy any manner Office or Fees within this Realm of England, Wales, or other the King's Dominion, upon Pain of forfeiting the same Offices or Fees, unless he or they use and exercise the English Speech or Language...

The wording of the document of the Acts of Union which came into force in 1536 and 1543. These laws made Wales a part of England and took away the status of Welsh and the right to use it in public life.

HISTORY GROUNDED

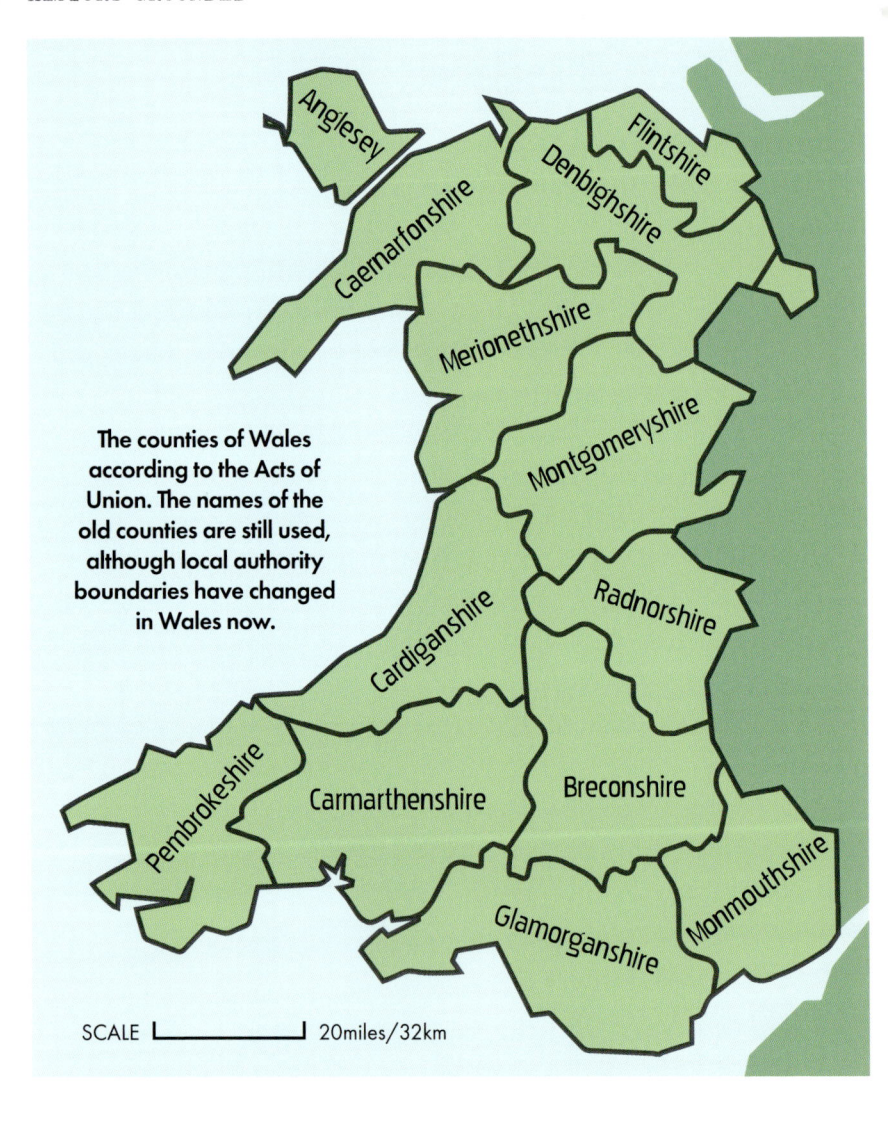

The counties of Wales according to the Acts of Union. The names of the old counties are still used, although local authority boundaries have changed in Wales now.

- Anglesey
- Flintshire
- Caernarfonshire
- Denbighshire
- Merionethshire
- Montgomeryshire
- Cardiganshire
- Radnorshire
- Pembrokeshire
- Carmarthenshire
- Breconshire
- Glamorganshire
- Monmouthshire

SCALE 20miles/32km

that affected everybody. There were no newspapers, no television or Google, and people are always much more interested in their own lives than anything else. At this time life was very uncertain and many people died of illnesses. If the harvest failed they might starve to death. So what was being done in London wasn't very interesting to most people. But, in fact, the changes that Henry VIII made so quickly would lead in time to changes in every part of people's lives.

HISTORY GROUNDED

DENBIGH

A. Henllan street
B. Chappell Lane
C. Sandy Lane
D. High Street
E. Lower Street
F. Love Lane
G. Parke Lane
H. Sowter Lane
I. The Chappell
K. The Abbey
L. The new church
M. Lenton Poole
N. The Castle
P. The way to ye Church

A Scale of paces

In 1610 John Speed made a famous map of the new counties of Wales and their county towns. The map above gives you a wonderful idea of what a town in Wales would have looked like in his time. As counties were established, so too were county towns — one town became the centre of local government and law and order. It is interesting to compare an old map, like the above of Denbigh, with today's aerial photograph (below). Sometimes the pattern of the streets, and their names, hasn't changed for centuries.

HISTORY GROUNDED

Two people from Tudor times

Bishop William Morgan (1545-1604)

In spite of the laws which made English the official language of Wales, many of us still speak Welsh today. Probably, that is because of one man's work. Latin was the language of the Catholic Church. That was the language of its services, its prayers and its publications, even though no one had spoken Latin as a living language for a thousand years. The Catholic Church did not want the Bible to be translated into the living languages of Europe.

As the power of the Catholic Church got weaker, scholars began to translate the Bible into all the different languages of Europe, including Welsh. Bishop William Morgan was mainly responsible for the Welsh translation. The aim was to make sure Welsh people learnt English by putting an English and a Welsh Bible in every church. But one result was that the beautiful Welsh of William Morgan's translation influenced everyone's Welsh for centuries, and gave them a wide vocabulary. The Welsh Bible is one of the first 15

Bishop William Morgan and the title page of his Bible, which was so important for the Welsh language

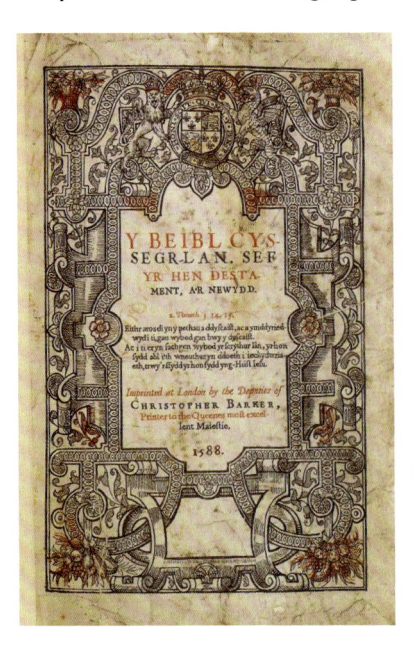

translations in the world, and from then on more and more books were published in Welsh.

William Morgan was born in Tŷ Mawr, Wybrnant, near Betws-y-coed. Although the house that stands there now was built a little after his time, it is still a good example of the home of a prosperous family in his time, with its thick, stone walls, its chimneys and its wide fireplaces.

Katheryn of Berain (1534-1591)

Katheryn was the daughter of a wealthy, noble family. She inherited lots of land in north Wales, and some beautiful big houses. Her father was a close friend of Henry VII, and was constable of Beaumaris castle. Katheryn was beautiful and clever, and fond of poetry. She was very close to the royal family too. In those days, every girl was expected to get married, and a lot of men wanted to marry her. Katheryn married four times, the first time in 1556 when she was 22 years old.

Her husband was John Salusbury, from another rich and important family in north Wales. They had two sons, but John died in 1566. The following year Katheryn married Sir Richard Clough, a very rich merchant. They had two daughters, and during their marriage they built Bach-y-graig and Plas Clough mansions – the first houses in Wales to be built of bricks.

But Richard died in 1570, and Katheryn was a rich widow for the second time. She married again, Maurice Wynn of Gwydir. They had two children as well – and once again Maurice died unexpectedly. By now Katheryn was one of the richest people in Britain. Her fourth – and last – husband was Edward Thelwall of Plas-y-ward. They had no children, and Katheryn died before Edward.

Katheryn of Berain

HISTORY GROUNDED

The architecture of the early gentry houses show imagination and money. Bach-y-graig in the Vale of Clwyd was the first house in Wales to be built of bricks. You can see that the parkland around Chirk Castle (below) was carefully planned – and expensive.

Katheryn had six children altogether, and she took care to marry them all "well" – that is, to the children of rich and important people. Katheryn had 16 grandchildren, and they were related to families all over Wales. Some people call her "Mam Cymru" – the mother of Wales.

Portmeirion is owned today by descendants of Katheryn and Richard Clough, and you can visit some of the beautiful houses she owned. Although she was so rich and important, nobody knows exactly where she is buried, but there is a strong tradition that she is buried in the graveyard at Llannefydd, Conwy.

Mansions and farmhouses

People in Wales who had enough money could be quite pleased with life in Tudor times. After all, a Welshman (of a sort) was king of England, welcoming Welsh people to his court – and giving them good jobs too. A lot of young men went to London to make their fortune. Their daring is the basis of the success of families like the Myddeltons of Chirk castle and the Cecils (the English version of the old Welsh name Seisyllt). This family has played an important part in politics since Dafydd Seisyllt caught Henry VII's attention and became an MP in 1504.

Although there was still a lot of fighting and violence at this time, there were no civil wars between 1485 and 1649, and this is the time when castles really did begin to become homes. The gentry also did well out of Henry VIII's decision to break away from the Catholic Church, and to close the monasteries. Although he took their riches for himself, he shared a lot of their lands with his friends. These were good days to be the king's friend, although it was so dangerous to be his wife! Some of the oldest mansions in Wales belong to this time, although there have been many changes to them over the centuries.

But one house has been put back to how it may have looked when it was built. Plas Mawr in Conwy was built between 1576 and 1585, in the time of Elizabeth I, the daughter of Henry VIII. Its first owner, Robert Wynn, didn't want to hide how rich he was, and the house is a colourful and unusual example of mansions of this time. Cadw have restored it,

Plas Mawr, Conwy

The Tudor Merchant's House, Tenby

A thatched cottage in Ceredigion

using the evidence we have now. You can wander through the whole house, from the kitchen (and the brewhouse) to the attics where the servants would sleep under a roof which is a masterpiece of enormous beams carved to fit together.

This is probably how other mansions from that time would have looked. There's not much of that original splendour to be seen today in Trebarried Hall, Powys, or Derwydd, near Llandeilo, or Althrey, Wrexham. And there are mansions just like these all over Wales, still showing us how good life was for some people in those days!

Poor people would have gone on building houses of wood and clay, houses which are easy and cheap to build. But they don't last long – and are really horrible to live in. Today there's almost nothing to be seen anywhere in Wales of miserable houses like that. You may have seen photographs of old thatched cottages with walls made out of straw and horse hair – but nobody lives in houses like that today. But sometimes, if you look carefully at a one-storey building at the side of a country road, you might see what's left of thatch under a corrugated iron roof. Yes, someone lived there once. Some of these old houses have been turned into outhouses on farms, or they have become sheds alongside a bigger house built later.

HISTORY GROUNDED

If you see a farmhouse built into the side of a hill, it's possible that it has foundations which are centuries old. In the times of the Tudors, and especially in the 17C, farmers who could afford it started to improve their houses. They turned mud walls into solid stone and put flagstones down on earth floors. Instead of the open fire that used to burn in the middle of the floor, they built chimneys on the end walls. They made separate rooms to sleep in, to cook and to wash clothes. Some of the houses you can see today in St Fagans National Museum of History belong to this period, for example Abernodwydd (1678) and Kennixton (1610).

Kennixton farmhouse, which is now in St Fagan's National Museum of History, was obviously the home of a wealthy farmer.

But if you want to see how the houses of earlier times might have looked, go to Hendre'r-ywydd Uchaf (1508), which is in the same museum – and remember that it too was a *mansion* in its day!

Markets and market towns

Farmers still take their animals and other produce from their farms to market to sell. And farmers' markets are popular today as a place to buy fresh food from the farmers rather than getting it in a supermarket. It's a place to meet people and to relax. That was true in the past as well, and the market square in the middle of a town would be full of stalls and pubs.

Some towns built whole halls for their markets. The old hall in Llanidloes still stands in the middle of the town, although it was built of wood sometime between 1612 and 1662. The Butter Market in Hay-on-Wye is newer: that was built in 1830, and a market is still held there every Thursday.

HISTORY GROUNDED

**A scene from a market in Aberystwyth;
(below) the old Butter Market at Hay-on-Wye**

A market was usually held every week. But some towns would hold a fair once or twice a year. This was a chance for people to look for work, and people would travel there to sell things that came from a long way away – exotic things local people couldn't produce. Fairs were held on open ground, and so there is nothing today to show where they happened.

Some farmers would arrange to take their cattle and sheep to markets in England as well. Drovers looked after the animals on their journey. They had to make sure they got a fair price for the farmer and bring the money back safely as well. This is how banks started, and the names of some banks show this. The Black Sheep Bank was founded at the end of the 18C, and the Black Ox Bank in Llandovery in 1799. Lloyds Bank bought the Black Ox business in 1909, but the old bank building still stands in the middle of the town.

The drovers' inn on Mynydd Epynt (top); an old photograph of two drovers (middle); a bank note from one of the drovers' banks (bottom)

Llandovery was one of the main meeting points for the drovers. You can walk some of the drovers' roads today, although some have vanished and lots of them take you over rough ground. For centuries, men would have taken hundreds of animals over these paths, with dogs to help them. If you are lucky, you might even find one of the cattle shoes, because their hooves had to be shod for their long journey.

Two pairs of cattle shoes which were in use at the time of the drovers

HISTORY GROUNDED

Fighting about religion

When you go to an old church – one built before 1500 – have a look at any statues there. If they were made before 1500, it's quite likely that they have been deliberately damaged – their eyes knocked out, or their noses broken away.

In the period after 1500 there was a lot of disagreement all across Europe about religion. Some people were faithful to the Catholic Church, accepting whatever the Pope said about religious matters, and they wanted everyone to agree with them. Other people believed that the Catholic Church had been leading people the wrong way for centuries, and they wanted everyone to agree with them that the Bible was the only important authority on religious matters.

There were religious wars everywhere in Europe in these centuries. Although Henry VIII had broken away from the Catholic Church, he hadn't changed much of what people believed. The ceremonies and celebrations that were such an important part of their lives hadn't changed either. But as time went on, more people began to doubt the teaching of the Catholic Church and to criticise its wealth. These disagreements would tear families

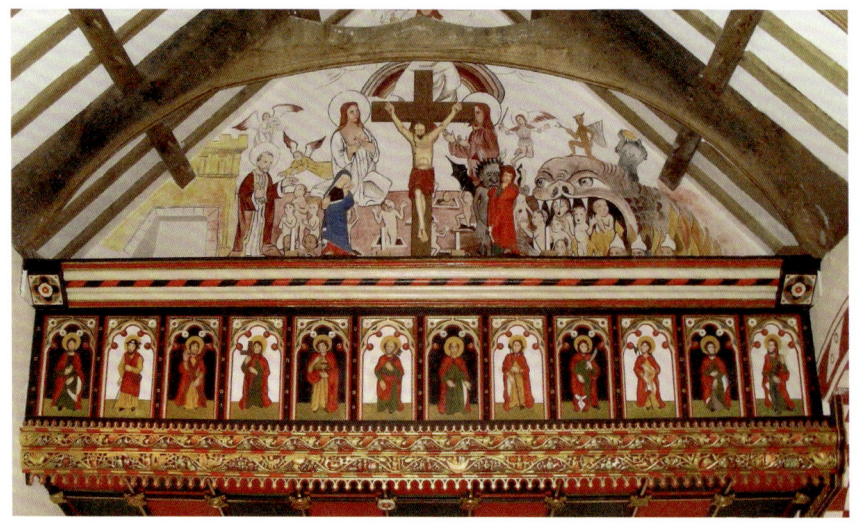

Some of the wall paintings from before the Protestant Reformation which have been recreated in the old church of St Teilo, Llandeilo Tal-y-bont, which has been moved to St Fagans

apart, and lead to one group persecuting and torturing the other.

There is often a secret room in mansions in Wales – somewhere to hide someone during a time of persecution.

There are memorials too that mark a place where someone was killed because of what they believed. Some of them are in very unexpected places.

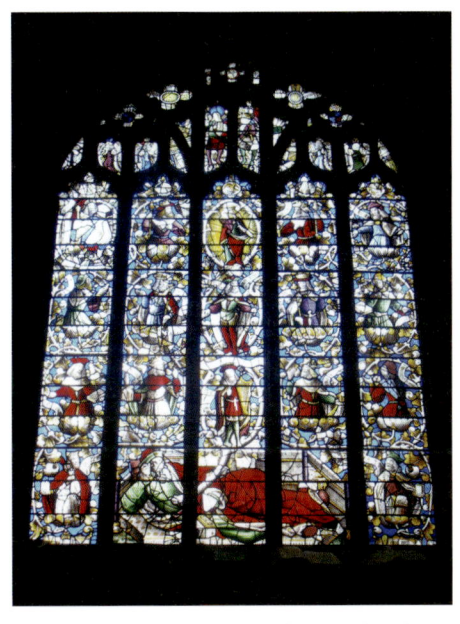

And every old church will have something to remind us of this time in history, like the amazing window in St Dyfnog's church, Llanrhaeadr-yng-Nghinmeirch, Denbighshire. It shows the tree of Jesse, which is the family tree of Jesus Christ. It was made about 1533, the year before Henry VIII broke away from the Catholic Church. Sometime during the years after that, a huge box was made for the window, so that it could be buried in the ground. It was put back in its place in the church in 1661.

The Jesse window, St Dyfnog's Church, Llanrhaeadr-yng-Nghinmeirch

A stone cross from the Catholic era at Patrishow church, Powys

At this time some people were turning against all church ceremonies. They were called Puritans or "Nonconformists" because they insisted on worshipping in a different way.

During the time of Elizabeth I the Anglican Church which her father had begun had developed a "middle way" between Catholicism and Puritanism. If people were willing to conform by attending their local church from time to time, the priests wouldn't question people too hard about what they believed. But in order to keep the country safe, it was decided that only members of the Anglican Church could have responsible jobs and could go to university. You had to conform to the Anglican Church if you wanted to be a Member of Parliament, or a Justice of the Peace, or even to have higher education.

Because of this, many Nonconformists made their careers in business. One group of them, the Quakers, wouldn't drink alcohol. But a number of them made fortunes by developing a new drink which had just come to Europe – chocolate. You will know the names of some of these families already: Cadbury, Terry, Fry, Rowntree. The Nonconformists set up their own schools to provide higher education. These academies taught new subjects like science, and new, revolutionary ideas would be discussed.

The memorial to Rawlins White, the Protestant martyr, in the middle of the House of Fraser shop, Cardiff

HISTORY GROUNDED

Chapels

The buildings of the Anglican Church are called churches, and many of them are in the shape of a cross, with a belfry or bell tower, because the church bell called people to services. The most important part of a church is the altar, where the priest gives communion to the worshippers. This is the central part of the church service.

The old chapel at Maesyronnen (below) and inside the "New Chapel", Nanhoron, Llŷn

   Chapels are usually oblong in shape, and the most important part is the pulpit. The sermon is the central part of the service in chapel, and the pulpit is high up, so that everyone can see and hear the preacher.

   The first chapels were very plain buildings, very like the barns where the early Nonconformists would often meet, in secret sometimes in the dangerous days of the 17C. Lots of huge, very grand chapels were built in Wales in the 19C. But sometimes you can see the simple building of the original chapel still standing in the shadow of the later big chapel.

Revolutions

The Pope and the Catholic Church had ruled every part of people's lives for centuries. But as people began to challenge their authority, they began to question other things that they had taken for granted for a long time too. The adventurous voyages of men like Columbus had shown how big the world was, and how many amazing things are in it.

Mathematical and scientific skills were developing at the same time. People began to find out more about the world around them, inventing experiments to test their ideas and theories. This is the beginning of the Scientific Revolution and the development of a scientific method of testing every theory against objective evidence.

One of the first sums we ever do is 1 + 1 = 2. Robert Recorde was a Welsh mathematician. He was born in Tenby about 1510. He was the one who invented the equals sign = which is used now all across the world.

Some of these experiments look very strange to us. But, by using this method of searching for knowledge, great discoveries were made – things which have made our world today. In the 17C, for example, the telescope, the pendulum and the barometer were invented. People worked out how blood circulates in our bodies, and how the laws of gravity work. This is the beginning of a process which is still going on today.

But, while these discoveries were being made, people began to question every sort of authority. They asked why it was that some people were rich and could live so well when other people found it so hard to live at all. When everyone was willing to accept that this was just God's will, it was possible to avoid these difficult questions. But once people realised that old customs and ways of thinking could be questioned, there began a time of questioning all authority.

A new freedom

Through the years, people had rebelled against their rulers for different reasons. But they were simply asking to be treated more fairly. They hadn't doubted that their rulers had the right to rule them. But that's what began to happen from the 17C on. To begin with, small groups of scholars would begin to discuss new ideas about the rights of common people. They said that reason was more important than custom as the basis for society's rules. They also began to put forward the revolutionary idea

A pamphlet celebrating the abolition of slavery

that everyone was born equal. These new ideas began to spread, and by the second half of the 18C many people were asking for a better society. They wanted old, unfair customs and privileges which were based just on the status or the wealth of your family to be done away with.

Slaves packing tobacco in Virginia

HISTORY GROUNDED

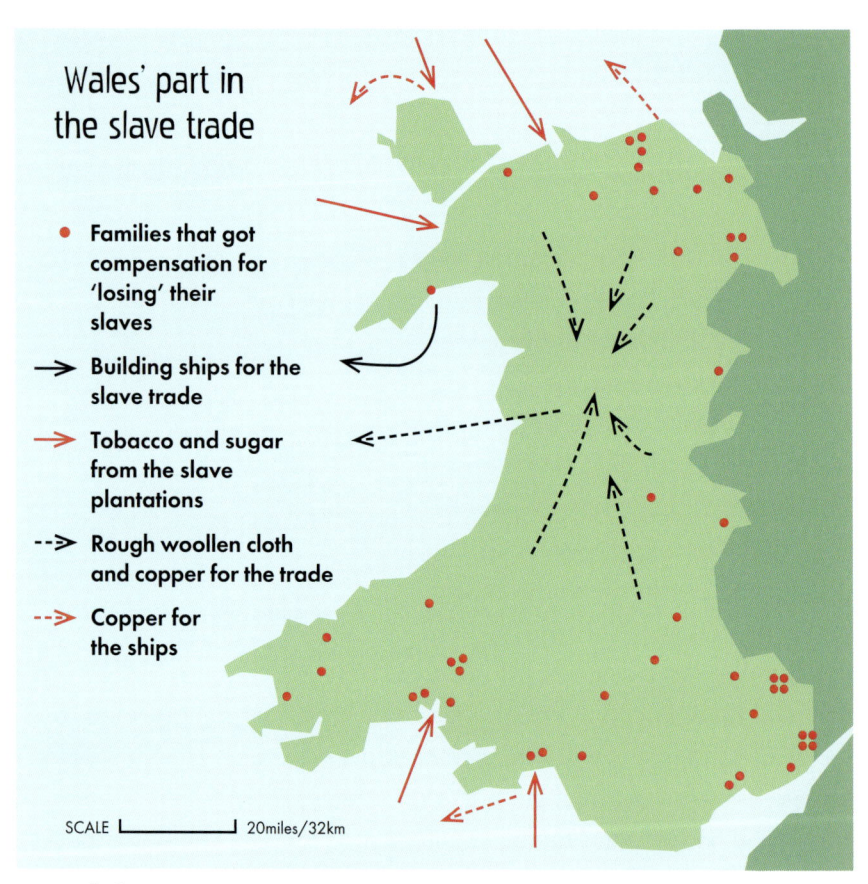

Wales' part in the slave trade

- Families that got compensation for 'losing' their slaves
- → Building ships for the slave trade
- → Tobacco and sugar from the slave plantations
- --> Rough woollen cloth and copper for the trade
- --> Copper for the ships

SCALE 20miles/32km

People began to campaign against the slave trade in the 18C. People like the Methodists hated it. They believed that God had made everyone equal and that everyone is one of God's children, no matter what the colour of their skin is. But there was a lot of opposition to this campaign. Although the campaigner William Wilberforce's bill to do away with slavery became law in 1833, the government had to pay compensation to the slave owners for a century and more.

There is a record of a ship from Barbados landing at Conwy harbour in 1740 with a cargo of sugar. This was one part of the trade triangle: ships would take goods like copper and the Welsh woollen cloth to Africa and use them to buy slaves there. Then the ships would take the slaves to the West Indies and America, and sell them there to buy cotton, sugar and tobacco to sell at home.

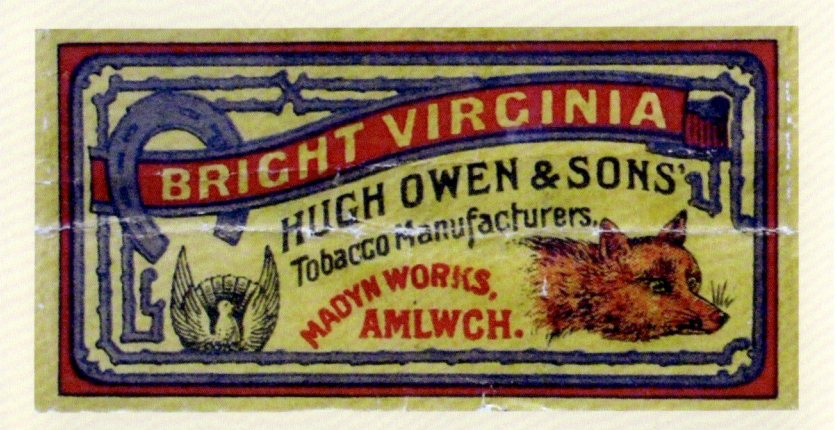

Amlwch was a busy harbour in the 18C. As well as exporting copper (which was used to make plates to protect the wooden hulls of the slave ships), it imported tobacco from the plantations in America.

Wales and the Slaves

Compensation money was paid to those who had owned slaves when the Slavery Abolition Act was passed in 1833 (see the map opposite). £20 million (£16 billion in today's money) was paid for the 800,000 slaves who were freed, and who had been the 'property' of 46,000 owners in Britain. Until 2015 British taxpayers' money was still being used to clear the government's debt after paying this compensation.

The records of the port of Pwllheli include these notes for 1801: "Ship Mary built to carry 600 slaves from Africa to America/A new chapel was built by the Calvinistic Methodists, Penmount Chapel".

The chapel and the ship were being built side by side on the quay - and the two were about the same size. The ship had been ordered by W. Courtney's shipyard (she was called 'Welsh Mary') for a Liverpool company, Forbes & Co.

Ann Griffiths (1776-1805)

Ann Griffiths never travelled far from her home, Dolwar-fach farm, which is near the village of Llanfihangel-yng-Ngwynfa in Powys. It isn't very far from Pennant Melangell. Ann was brought up in the Anglican Church. But when she was a young girl she started to going to the meetings being held by a particular group within that church. This group was getting

A carved image of Ann Griffiths' head

a lot of attention because of their fiery sermons and their calls for a new spirit in church services. They wanted a more emotional spirit which emphasised a person's direct relationship with God. They called themselves "Methodists" because they followed a method of reading the Bible, prayer and reflection. Ann became a full member of this group when she was twenty.

In 1804, Ann married a young man called Thomas Griffiths, and he came to live at Dolwar-fach. Before long Ann was expecting a baby. Having a baby could be very dangerous in those days. Her daughter Elizabeth was born on 13 July, but she died very soon, and was buried on 31 July. Ann died soon afterwards and was buried on 12 August.

This is a short, sad story – and the story of many women over the centuries because of the dangers of having babies. So why then do we remember Ann Griffiths? Because she wrote wonderful religious poetry, hymns which are remembered and still sung today, 200 years after she wrote them. They are about serious religious ideas and show a detailed knowledge of the Bible, but there are deep feelings in them too.

According to the story, Ann would compose these poems after a time of reflection and prayer. She would sing them then with joy and triumph. But she would only do this at home, and in the company of her maidservant Ruth, who was also her close friend. Ruth couldn't write, but she learnt the verses by heart. She would recite them to her husband, so that he could write them down and keep them safe. This is the only reason why we know about the wonderful work of Ann Griffiths.

HISTORY GROUNDED

Iolo Morganwg (1747-1826)

Iolo Morganwg (Edward Williams) was an imaginative antiquarian. He worked as a stonemason, and travelled the length and breadth of Wales and beyond, collecting information about old standing stones and stone circles. He collected old manuscripts too, and invented many new Welsh words for the new inventions and ideas of his time. He was a creative genius, and, like others at that time, didn't think there was anything wrong in creating "old" manuscripts and papers to back up his ideas. One of his ideas was that Welsh poetry belonged to an ancient tradition which went back to Celtic times. He set up Gorsedd y Beirdd, an association of poets to celebrate and protect this tradition. He invented some strange ceremonies for them, and the plaque shown below at Primrose Hill, London, was put there to mark where the first meeting of the Gorsedd was held in 1792. He was inspired by the ideas of the French Revolution – he called himself "The Poet of Freedom" – and argued against slavery.

Iolo Morganwg and the plaque to commemorate him at Primrose Hill, London

HISTORY GROUNDED

Owain Glyndŵr's Mount near Glyndyfrdwy, Corwen –
the location of one of his courts

A MYSTERY IN THE GROUND
Where is Glyndŵr's grave?

Nobody knows to this day where Glyndŵr is buried. There are lots of different ideas about what might have happened to him after Harlech castle was captured in 1409. One thing is certain: Glyndŵr wasn't in the castle. He wasn't taken prisoner to England either. He had a big family, and a lot of faithful friends too. Did they look after him? Or did he hide away somewhere in the mountains of Wales? No-one knows for certain.

But new evidence for the past is always being found, and we have new ways of studying it too. In 2012 scientists proved that it was the bones of King Richard III that had been found in the earth under a car park in Leicester. He had been killed in 1485. They used the new technique of analysing DNA. Maybe someone will find Glyndŵr's grave one day - and be able to prove it!

HISTORY GROUNDED

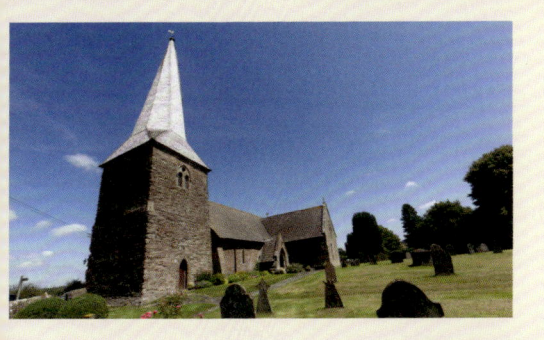

Here are three places where, according to experts, Owain Glyndŵr might be buried: Abbey Cwm-hir; Monnington-on-Wye church, and Kimbolton church

HISTORY GROUNDED

1600		1700	
Early industry about 1640	The growth of ports about 1750	Steam engine 1804	

Dates

Part 3: Timeline

Questions

- What were the first industries in Wales?
- What advantages did the sea have for Wales?
- Why was Richard Trevithick's work so important?

HISTORY GROUNDED

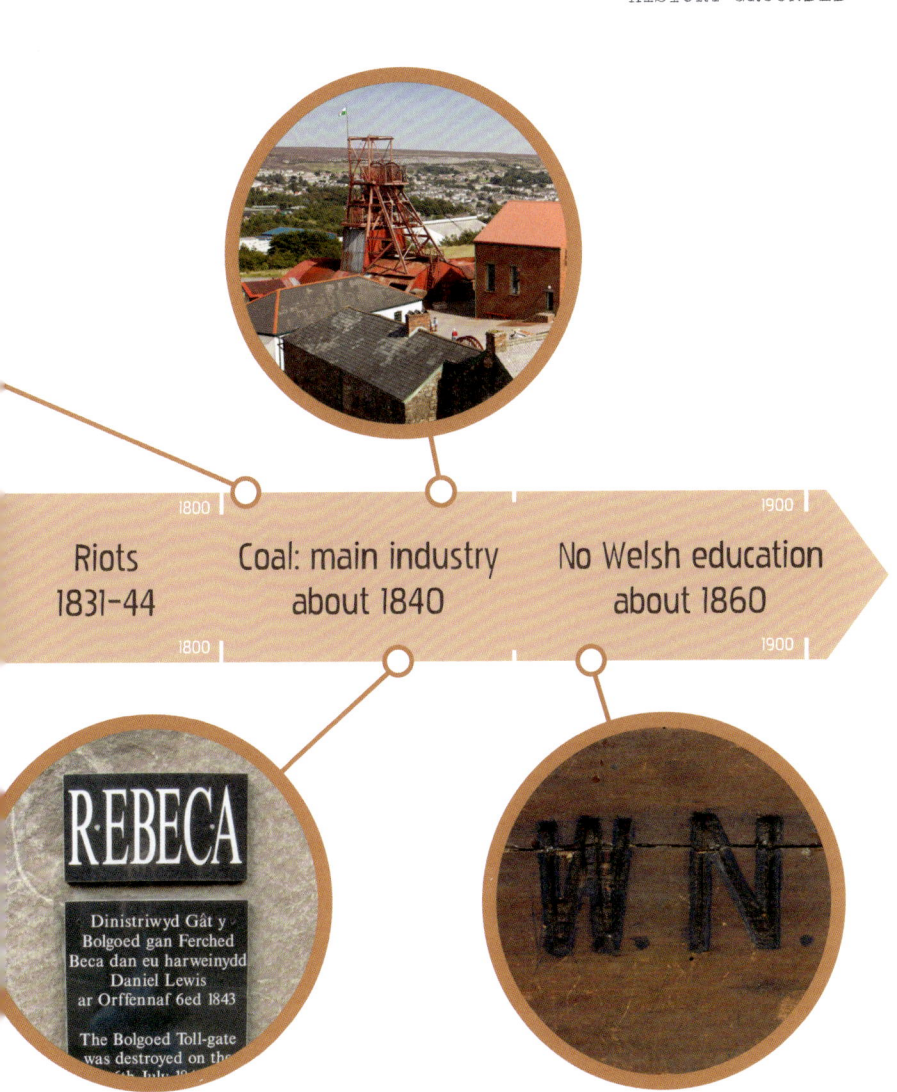

| 1800 | | 1900 |
| Riots 1831–44 | Coal: main industry about 1840 | No Welsh education about 1860 |

REBECA

Dinistriwyd Gât y Bolgoed gan Ferched Beca dan eu harweinydd Daniel Lewis ar Orffennaf 6ed 1843

The Bolgoed Toll-gate was destroyed on the...

W. N.

- Why did people raise a red flag in Merthyr?
- How good was life for miners' families?
- What part did schools play in making Welsh people speak English?

123

HISTORY GROUNDED

Early mining in Wales in the 16C and 17C

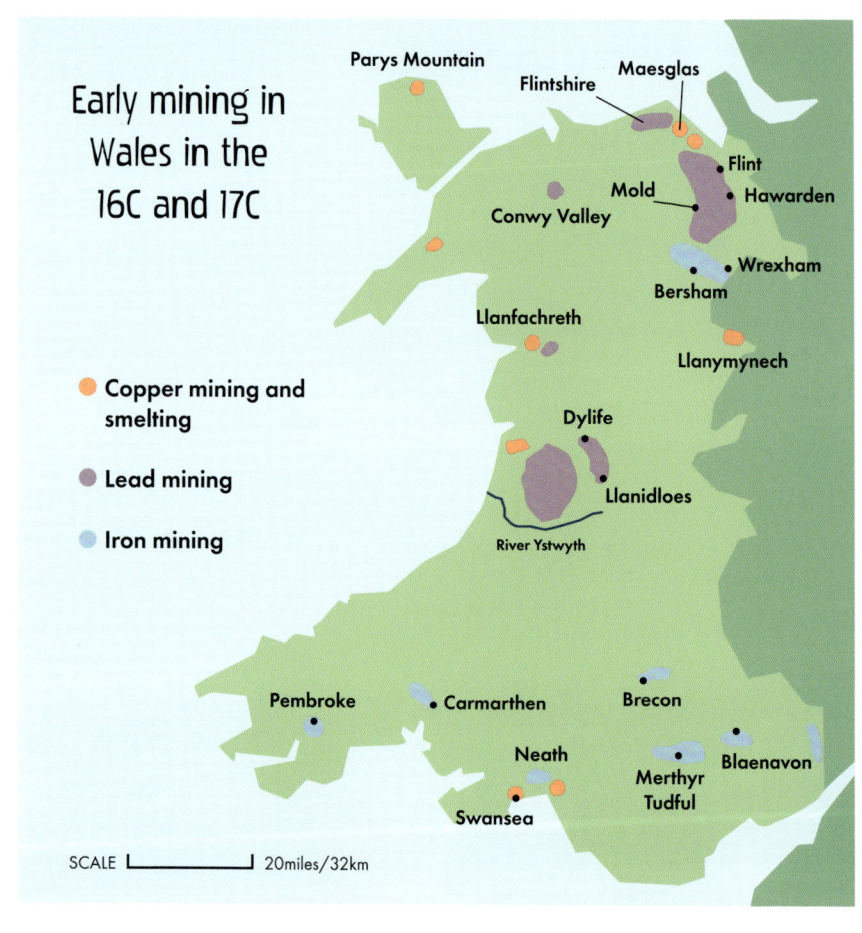

- **Copper mining and smelting**
- **Lead mining**
- **Iron mining**

Locations: Parys Mountain, Flintshire, Maesglas, Mold, Flint, Hawarden, Conwy Valley, Wrexham, Bersham, Llanfachreth, Llanymynech, Dylife, Llanidloes, River Ystwyth, Pembroke, Carmarthen, Brecon, Neath, Merthyr Tudful, Blaenavon, Swansea

SCALE 20 miles/32km

After the time of the first farmers, the forests weren't cut down for centuries, and there were lots of trees in Wales. Then, as industry developed in the 16C, they began to be cut down to make charcoal for the early iron furnaces.

An unknown poet of the 16C wrote a long poem in Welsh protesting against the destruction of Cwm Cynon woods, and here are two verses translated into English:

Glyn Cynon Woods

Aberdare, all of Llanwynno,
Merthyr parish as far as Llanfabon,
The worst of all
Was cutting down Glyn Cynon Woods.

Many a birch tree in its green cloak
(May the English be hanged!)
Is now one huge bonfire
For the men of the black iron.

Early Industry in Wales

People have been working the metals that are found in the ground in Wales for thousands of years. But by now there's not much left to see of those early industries. Mining destroys the evidence for itself, buildings become ruins, and plants grow over the sites. For example, the area around Blaenavon, in the south-east, is listed as one of the most important heritage sites in the world. But there is very little to see now on the bare hills above the town to show that people have been mining metal there for a thousand years. You need an expert to help you find the remains of the old workings.

But, from the time of Elizabeth I onwards, some families got very rich by developing metal mines and coal pits. There had been a coal mine in Mostyn, Flintshire, for example, since 1294. But when Sir Roger Mostyn bought the mine in 1602 he began to extend the workings by sinking new pits. Before long this was the biggest coal mine in Wales. The same

Early mining machines in the shaft of Mostyn colliery (left) and the site of that colliery today at the mouth of the river Dee (right)

HISTORY GROUNDED

sort of thing happened with the iron industry in the north-east of Wales at the same time. There were ironworks at Bersham in 1640, and, according to one story, weapons were made here for the civil war between the king and parliament (1642–1651).

The remains of old workings like these can be seen in different parts of Wales: lead in Flintshire and Ceredigion, iron in the valleys of the south, copper on Parys Mountain in Anglesey. There were workings wherever metals could be found without digging too far underground. There were no safe ways of lighting deep mines, or getting fresh air into them. In the same way, small coal pits would be sunk wherever the coal was near the surface of the ground. They used to dig into the ground there and get as much coal out as they could before the earth began to collapse into the hole. So, everything was quite small in those days. Things would change, as we will see.

The remains of Bersham ironworks today

Old lime kilns on Halkyn Mountain

HISTORY GROUNDED

The remains of the copper mines on Parys Mountain, Anglesey

A drawing of early smelting in the old abbey at Neath

127

HISTORY GROUNDED

Sir Humphrey Mackworth (1657-1727)

Sir Humphrey was born in Shropshire. When he married Mary Evans of Neath, who had inherited all her father's lands and riches, Sir Humphrey became the owner of the rights to work minerals in the area. Coal had been mined there for years, but Sir Humphrey decided to develop the local copper mines, using coal to melt the copper.

Sir Humphrey was ready to try out new ideas, to experiment with new methods and to expand his business. He was responsible for the first mines in Ceredigion in 1698, and in 1704 he set up a company called The Company of Mines Adventurers. He was one of the first to use wooden rails to make it easier to move drams of coal and minerals in his works. This is the beginning of railways, which became so important later on – a century after Sir Humphrey himself died. He also experimented with the idea of putting sails on his drams to use wind power to move the loads. That wasn't so successful, but it does show how willing people like Sir Humphrey were to try something new and to experiment.

Underground in Cwmystwyth lead mine. You can clearly see the Roman level on the left.

But not every experiment works: Sir Humphrey's company failed in 1709. He went on trying to develop his works, but he had other interests as well. Like other rich men he was a Member of Parliament. At that time people like him could agree between themselves who would be elected to Parliament. Only rich people were allowed to vote in those days. Some of Sir Humphrey's descendants became Members of Parliament too.

Sir Humphrey was a religious man, and he helped to set up the Society for the Promotion of Christian Knowledge (SPCK). He gave money to the society, and to set up two schools for the children of his workers, one in Esgair Hir, Ceredigion, and the other in Neath. And as well as all that, he wrote several religious books.

HISTORY GROUNDED

The remains of the old mine workings at Cwmystwyth

Old iron furnaces at Stepaside, Pembrokeshire

HISTORY GROUNDED

The bridge at Bangor-on-Dee, Wrexham, which was built in 1603. Wrexham has been an important industrial town for centuries.

Travel and communication

As industry began to develop in Wales in the 16C and 17C, some rich people began to take advantage of this by building bridges to make travelling easier. These would make it easier to move the things their works were producing. Some of these old bridges are still standing, and are very beautiful. But they also tell us how busy and important that area was in the time they were built.

For centuries, every community had to look after its own roads. Although that sounds quite fair, a lot depends on how many people, animals and vehicles travel over those roads. If you lived in the country, only people from your community would probably be using the roads regularly. But what if you lived near a town or an important port, or near a mine or ironworks? Shouldn't those strangers who were using your roads help to pay the cost of keeping them safe?

By the end of the 17C, Parliament was starting to take responsibility for looking after the main roads, by setting up turnpike companies. Every company would put a gate across the road, with a house beside it for the man who looked after the gate. Every traveller would have to pay to have the gate opened. This money was used to repair the road. People liked this way of maintaining the most important roads. You could make a profit by charging a lot of money.

A turnpike house on the A5 near Llangollen is still someone's home today

After all, everybody had to use the road. Hundreds of different turnpike companies were set up across the country in the 18C, and it's easy to spot an old turnpike house because of its unique shape. Some of these companies competed with each other, and put lots of gates across roads leading to important towns. So there are lots of these old turnpike houses to be seen throughout Wales.

A safer way of carrying heavy goods was to use rivers. But there

Llanrwst bridge (above), built in 1636 to link Caernarfonshire and Denbighshire; Presteigne bridge (right) which crosses the river Lugg, the boundary between Wales and England here. How many place names are there in Wales with "pont/bont" in them? The List of Historic Places website lists over 5,000 – this shows how important bridges are everywhere.

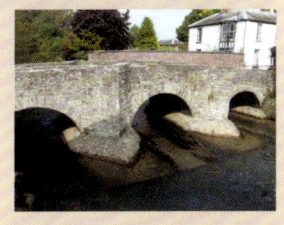

HISTORY GROUNDED

Nantgarw Pottery beside the convenient canal which was completed in 1794 (left); the canal beside the lime quarry at Llanymynech (right)

weren't many rivers in Wales that were suitable for doing this. In the 18C too people began to experiment with artificial rivers – canals. Like turnpike roads, canals became very popular, especially for carrying heavy minerals like iron and coal to the nearest port. They were also a safe way of carrying much more expensive and fragile things. China works making very high standard porcelain were set up in Swansea and Nantgarw, partly because there were canals close by.

The Pontcysyllte Aqueduct carrying the Llangollen canal across the river Dee (it was opened in 1805)

A painting of Aberystwyth harbour, between 1880 and 1899

Wales and the sea

When you look at a map of Wales, you can see the country has four sides. One of them is the border between Wales and England in the east. But the sea is the border on the other three sides, in the north, west and south. All along this long coast there are lots of sheltered bays, river mouths and other convenient places for ships. It's not a long journey by sea to Ireland in the west, to the Isle of Man and Scotland in the north, and to England and Brittany in the south. So, it's not very surprising that every seaside village in Wales used to be a port. In those days travel by sea, although it could be dangerous, was quicker and often safer than travel over land.

The ports of Wales have a long history, and you can see the marks of that history very clearly, even in little villages like Cwmtudu in Ceredigion and Borth-y-gest in Gwynedd. Look for a lime kiln on the beach: ships

HISTORY GROUNDED

Unloading a boat on the beach at Porth Ysgaden, Llŷn (left); iron mooring ring for boats at Borth-y-gest, near Porthmadog (right)

would bring loads of limestone to the shore. The limestone would be burnt in the kiln to turn it into fertiliser for the farms. In days gone by the beach would have been a busy place: sailing ships unloading on the beach, and rows of horses and carts waiting to carry the lime to the farms.

Other goods would be brought into these small ports, and the produce of local farms would be exported. Look for iron rings in harbour walls where ships would be tied up. In some places you can see grooves in the rocks – the marks left by centuries of cartwheels.

The top of an old kiln, Porth Ysgaden, Llŷn (left); Cwmtudu kiln, Ceredigion (right). As more and more industries developed in Wales, more and more food needed to be produced. Spreading lime on the soil made it better for growing grass for animals.

134

The story of Wales and the sea has some colourful stories about pirates too, like Sir Harry Morgan and Black Bart. But there is a dark side to the close link between Wales and the sea. It wasn't only goods that were the cargo of some Welsh ships. In the past, people were carried on ships, to be bought and sold like goods. This was the cruel slave trade. For centuries ships sailed from Europe down to Africa. There the sailors would use cheap goods from Europe to buy people as slaves. Then they would be taken across the Atlantic to be sold in the Caribbean islands and in other parts of America. These slaves would work on the sugar plantations. It was possible to sell sugar and rum, the spirit that is made from it, for a high price home in Europe.

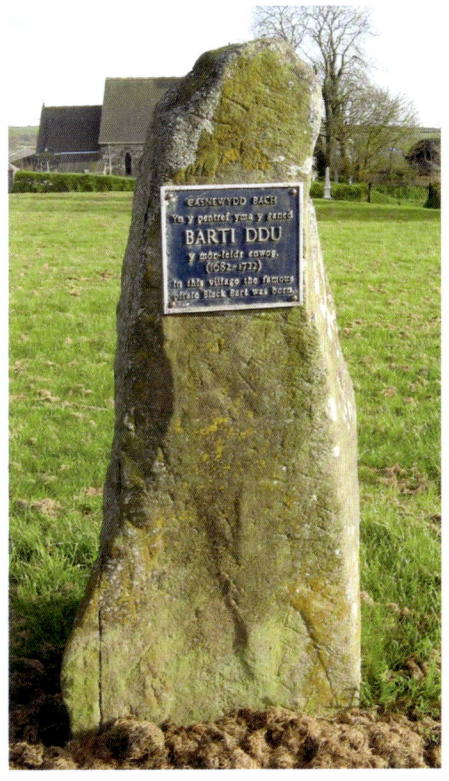

A memorial stone to the pirate Barti Ddu ("Black Bart") at Little Newcastle, Pembrokeshire

By now we understand how horrible and cruel the slave trade was. But it was the basis of the wealth of the Pennant family, who owned the Penrhyn slate quarries in Bethesda, Gwynedd. Richard Crawshay used the money he had made in the slave trade to set up the big ironworks in Cyfarthfa, Merthyr Tudful. These weren't the only people who got rich this way. Many famous families in Wales made their fortunes from this trade, and the profits supported hundreds of families and businesses across the country.

HISTORY GROUNDED

The coal, slate, tin, wool, silver, lead and gold industries in 1850

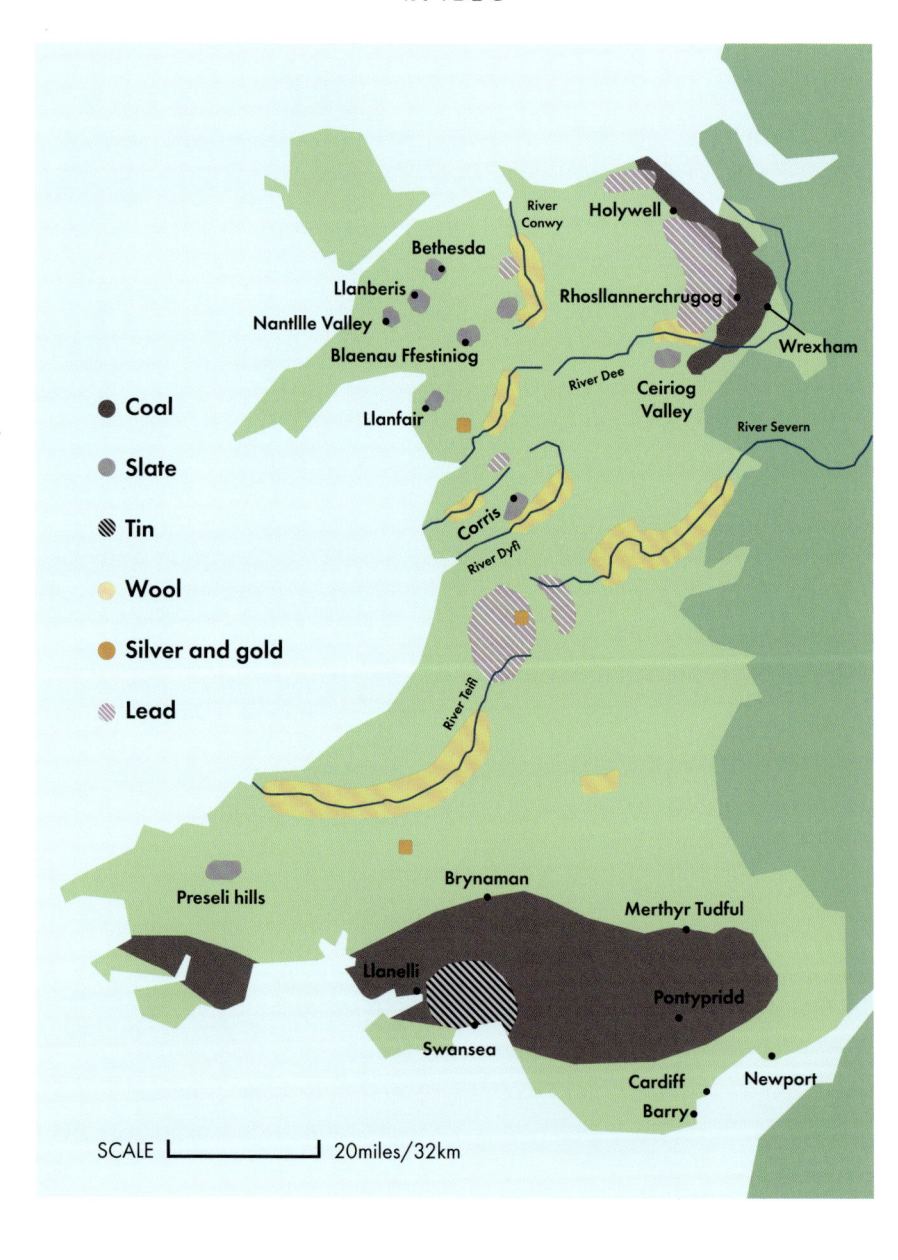

HISTORY GROUNDED

Industrialising Wales

In the middle of the 18C several things come together to change the lives of Welsh people, and to change the sort of marks they would leave on their country. The turnpike road and the canals made it easier to travel and to move goods, especially heavy things like iron, coal, building stone and slates. Think of the difference between loading stones onto a row of ponies and then leading them over rough roads in bad weather – and loading the same stones on to a canal boat. It only took one horse on its own to pull a boat carrying the same weight along a canal.

A new way of carrying goods had developed too. People had begun to put long pieces of wood on either side of the road to let cartwheels move more smoothly over a rough or muddy road. That worked well, and a network of dramroads developed in the coal and metal mines.

To get power, most industries still depended on ways that had been used for thousands of years – the strength of people and animals, and the power of wind and water. Wales has a lot of streams and rivers – and plenty of rain to feed them – and is also a windy country. So, watermills and windmills used to be very common across the whole of Wales.

You can see their remains everywhere. At one time there were over 90 windmills in Wales – 49 of them just in Anglesey.

Horses pulling slate waggons in the quarries above Blaenau Ffestiniog

A large waterwheel is the background to this photograph, taken around 1885, of men, women and boys in the slate enamelling works, Tywyn, Meirionnydd. You often see a dog in old photographs of people at work. Rats were – and are – very common!

And there were hundreds of watermills in Wales! Over 200 of these are still standing, and have been registered as historic buildings. Place names like Melin Newydd ("New Mill"), Hen Felin ("Old Mill"), y Felinheli (maybe "the mill by the sea" or "the mill on the river Heulyn"), Melin Gruffudd ("Gruffudd's mill") are clues to help you find these old mills. The mill was very important to the community. Every farmer had to have the corn he grew in his fields ground in the mill before he could use it or sell it as flour, and power was needed to full or finish the woollen cloth produced by the sheep farms. Place names like Pandy Tudur, in the Conwy Valley, and Tonypandy, Rhondda Valley, tell us there used to be a *pandy* ("fulling mill") for woollen cloth there.

Many of the watermills are ruins now, or have been turned into people's homes, or into something else, like part of a factory. But look for the millstones from the old corn mills – they are very hard to destroy – or to move!

HISTORY GROUNDED

Llynnon Mill, Anglesey, was restored to work again in 1976 – the only windmill still working in Wales today.

The ruins of an old mill at Tre-fin, Pembrokeshire

An old painting of a watermill, Swyddffynnon, Ceredigion

A millstone in a museum at Cenarth, Carmarthenshire

The wheel of an old mill at Aber-arth, Ceredigion

HISTORY GROUNDED

But at the beginning of the 19C a new form of power was developing. As early as 1698 Thomas Savery had realised that the power of steam could be controlled and used to work the pumps that raised water out of mine workings. Steam was much more powerful than the old ways of powering machines, and it was more reliable than water or wind.

In 1804 a young man from Cornwall called Richard Trevithick had tried out a new idea. He used steam power to pull drams laden with iron along the tramway from Merthyr Tudful to Abercynon in Cwm Taf. This was the beginning of a new period in the history of industry – the time of railways and steam engines.

From the 1830s on, steam engines began to be used to pull a train of waggons carrying people as well as goods. A network of railways were built very quickly to link towns together, and for the first time in history people began to travel faster than horses.

This new way of travelling would change the world – and time. Before the railways came, people kept time by the sun, which sets later in the west than the east, but now every clock in the country had to keep the same time. A train moves faster across land than the sun moves across the sky.

Richard Trevithick's engine recreated – this copy is in the National Waterfront Museum, Swansea

The growth of industry in the 19C

Every industry in Wales developed very quickly in the 19C, and the size and the power of the works grew as well. Thousands and thousands of people came from all over the country to these works, and villages like Merthyr Tudful grew into big towns in a few years. According to the 1801 census, 7,705 people were living there; there were 22,000 there by the 1831 census, and 46,000 by 1851. By then, Merthyr Tudful was the biggest town in Wales.

This is the most striking example, but the same thing was true of the other industrial parts of Wales – as the work grew, so did the population.

A steam engine taking a load of bricks along a tramway in a brickworks in Flintshire

HISTORY GROUNDED

Population of the Welsh Counties, 1801-1901

County	1801	1821	1841	1861	1881	1901
Anglesey	33,806	45,063	50,891	54,609	51,416	50,606
Brecknock	32,325	43,826	55,603	61,627	57,746	54,213
Caernarfon	41,521	58,099	81,093	95,694	119,349	123,481
Cardigan	42,956	57,784	68,766	72,245	70,270	61,078
Carmarthen	67,317	90,239	106,326	111,796	124,864	135,328
Denbigh	60,299	76,428	88,478	100,078	111,740	131,582
Flint	39,469	53,893	66,919	69,737	80,587	81,485
Glamorgan	70,879	102,073	171,188	317,753	511,433	860,510
Meirionnydd	29,506	34,382	39,332	38,963	52,038	48,852
Monmouth	45,568	75,801	134,368	174,633	211,267	297,497
Montgomery	48,184	60,245	69,607	66,919	65,718	54,901
Pembroke	56,280	73,788	88,044	96,278	91,824	87,894
Radnor	19,135	22,533	25,458	25,382	23,528	23,281
Wales	587,245	794,154	1,046,073	1,312,834	1,571,780	2,012,876

Reference Wales, John May (University of Wales Press, 1994, tt. 18-19)

Since 1801, a census has been held by the government every ten years. Every person living in the country has to be counted on the night of the census. You can learn much about the past from the results of the census. This table clearly shows the growth of Glamorgan's population between 1801 and 1901.

Wales had been a land of small towns, of villages and farms until the end of the 18C. In 1770 only about 500,000 people lived in Wales. By 1851, 1,163,000 were living here. There was a huge growth in the number of people living in some parts of Wales – especially in the counties of Glamorgan and Monmouthshire in the south and the Wrexham area in the north.

The industries in one of the south Wales valleys in 1825 through the eyes of artist Penry Williams

The big industries

Between 1800 and 1900 some of the big industries changed Wales, and you can clearly see their mark on the landscape today. Look for the heaps of waste material, for the ruins of the works and the towns and villages that were built for the workers. These industries left their mark on the environment and on the health of the workers and their families.

You can still see the huge scar the copper industry left on Anglesey, at Parys Mountain, 200 years after that industry finished. In the 1780s this was the most important copper mine in the world, but by 1831 only a handful of miners were still there, because the copper ore was gone. But the

Underground tunnels in the old copper workings, Sygun, Beddgelert

enormous hole is still there today, showing us what incredible work went on there. All that work was done by hand – pick and shovel work, and a lot of this heavy work was done by women – the copper ladies – and children, as well as men.

By 1800, the ironworks at Merthyr Tudful and Blaenavon were growing fast. The iron ore was close to the surface of the ground in that area, and there had been iron furnaces there for hundreds of years. But now, new ways of working the metal were being invented, using coal instead of wood in the furnaces. There was plenty of coal there too, as well as the limestone that was used in the furnaces to improve the quality of the iron, and water to work the machines. Adventurous men like Richard Crawshay made fortunes in Merthyr. Castell Cyfarthfa, the home of that family, still looks across at the site of the Cyfarthfa ironworks. You can still see the ruins of the enormous furnaces there today.

HISTORY GROUNDED

An iron furnace in Merthyr

Thousands came to work in these industries. Though the work was so dangerous, the money was good! Houses had to be built for the workers, and slate – a type of stone found in some parts of Wales – is excellent for making good roofs. There are roofs all across the world that have come from Welsh slate quarries. Most of these quarries were in Gwynedd. The Penrhyn quarries in Bethesda and Dinorwig quarries in Llanberis were the two biggest slate quarries in the world. You can see the cliff faces where the quarrymen would work in the open air. And you can fly over the quarry itself on a zipwire! Your heart will beat fast, but think of the danger of the work itself. In the Ffestiniog area, the slate was worked in underground mines, and you have to go 500 feet/152 metres underground to see how quarrymen worked there in conditions which were just as difficult, hard and dangerous.

Other metals, like gold, silver and lead had been mined for centuries

HISTORY GROUNDED

too, and you can see the remains of these works today. You can visit the mines at Dolaucothi, Carmarthenshire, where miners have been looking for gold from Roman times to 1938. Other metals which aren't as beautiful as gold were in the ground in Wales too. You can see ruins of lead and silver mines in the countryside at Bryntail, Powys; Cwmystwyth, Ceredigion, and Halkyn Mountain, Flint. These were important centres of industry in their day too.

But coal was the giant among all these industries. At first, all the other industries needed coal, as fuel for the furnaces which melted the ore, and then they needed it for the new steam engines. As well as that, people

The Oakeley quarry, Blaenau Ffestiniog – one of the biggest quarry workings in the world, with the lowest workings below sea level

A woman working in the Clayton tin works, Pontarddulais. Many women did heavy work in the different industries. They would carry coal and pull drams in the pits, and break up the copper ore with hammers at Parys Mountain, Anglesey, and Drws-y-coed, Llanllyfni

HISTORY GROUNDED

Big Pit National Coal Museum

wanted coal to heat all the new buildings. And there was plenty of coal to be had in the valleys of south Wales. Rows of houses were built along the sides of these narrow valleys, and you can still see many of these today. The coal mines themselves have gone, and most of the waste tips have been cleared away, but the houses and the people are still here.

Coal was sent all over the world from ports like Cardiff, Newport, Barry and Swansea, and the grand buildings you can see there are proof of the

Miners' Institute, Rhosllannerchrugog

Terraced houses, New Tredegar, Rhymney Valley

HISTORY GROUNDED

Mothers with their children waiting for news at the pithead in Senghennydd in October 1913. There had been an explosion and a fire in the mine. A total of 440 men and boys were killed that day. Many had moved there from all parts of Wales to find work and better pay. This is the worst industrial accident in British history.

wealth and the importance of the industry. The majestic Coal Exchange building in the docks area of Cardiff was built in 1883 as a centre for buying and selling the coal which was being exported to the four corners of the world – in steamships that also used coal. In 1913, 37 million tons of coal were exported from here – and 98.8% of it had been cut by hand.

People from the four corners of the world came to live in the streets of these ports. Multi-ethnic communities grew up in the docks areas. The Norwegian church near the Senedd reminds us of the tons of wood imported to Wales for the industry, and of adventurous sailors from Norway like Roald Dahl's father. If you walk around the church, you will see words for many different languages carved into the stones beside you. These are examples of all the different languages you would have heard in these docks when Cardiff was the capital city of King Coal!

HISTORY GROUNDED

A statue of a coal-mining family in Llwynypia. Coal-mining was always dangerous – for the miner and his wife. Nearly half of all the fatal accidents that happened in British mines between 1880 and 1900 were in the Welsh coalfield. There were many more non-fatal accidents, which might make it impossible for a man to work again. The health of the miners' wives suffered even more, because of poor care and the endless hard, physical work of keeping the house clean. The coal dust was in the air everywhere.

How people lived in the industrial towns

All these people had to have homes to live in, and the new towns had to be kept clean too. The old ways of doing this couldn't cope with the new demands. The result of this was that the living and working conditions of the industrial towns and villages was dreadful, dirty and dangerous to health. More than one family would live in the same house, and they would take in lodgers too. Several houses would share the same toilet, and very often you had to walk a long way to get water for washing and cooking.

The old ways of organising society had to change. But, unfortunately, ordinary working people had no voice in how the country was run, or how to make their working and living conditions better. People became angry and frustrated, and they showed this by protesting. These protests would often turn into riots. That's what happened in Merthyr Tudful in 1831.

DIC PENDERYN
CANED RICHARD LEWIS   BORN RICHARD LEWIS
YM 1808 YN ABERAFAN   IN 1808 IN ABERAVON
CROGWYD yn NGHARCHAR   AND HANGED AT CARDIFF
CAERDYDD AR AWST 13-1831   GAOL ON AUGUST 13TH 1831
AR OL Y TERFYSG YM   FOLLOWING THE MERTHYR
MERTHYR YR UN FLWYDDYN   INSURRECTION OF THAT YEAR
MERTHYR GWEITHWYR CYMRU   A MARTYR OF THE WELSH

Dic Penderyn – a plaque on Carnegie Library, Merthyr Tudful

In 1831 in Merthyr Tydfil, South Wales, employees of the merciless Ironmaster William Crawshay and townspeople took to the streets to protest at unemployment and working conditions. It is believed that this was the first time the red flag of revolution was raised. Twenty-four protesters were killed, many more imprisoned or transported, and one innocent, Dic Penderyn, hanged for allegedly stabbing a soldier. The notorious event became known as the

MERTHYR RISING

A drawing of the Red Flag being raised for the first time ever in Merthyr in 1831. It became the banner of workers' protests throughout the world from then on.

HISTORY GROUNDED

The campaign for the vote

In 1830 Parliament was discussing the possibility of letting more people have the chance of voting for someone to speak for them in Parliament. From the beginning, only men who owned land had the right to vote. There were a few exceptions – for example, in some towns people had inherited the right to vote – but most people didn't have a vote at all, and the whole system was very shaky. Votes could be bought, and you had to vote in public. This old system favoured wealthy people.

But although many people wanted to change things, and to make the system fairer, many others were afraid of this, believing it would lead to a bloody revolution. But people had already begun to revolt. A protest in Merthyr Tudful in 1831 turned into fierce fighting, and many people were killed. There was no police force in those days, and the only way the government could stop the fighting was to send soldiers in to frighten the rioters and to shoot at them too.

Cyfarthfa Castle, where the Crawshay family lived. They owned some of the biggest ironworks in Merthyr.

A law to reform Parliament was passed in 1832, but many were disappointed in it. Riots went on happening across Britain, and in 1836 the People's Charter was published. This asked for several improvements, including giving the vote to all men over 21 and making sure it was possible to vote in private. A petition was organised to present to Parliament, asking the members to accept the Charter. But Parliament refused this request, and every other request afterwards to make the People's Charter the law of the land.

HISTORY GROUNDED

Memorials to the Rebecca Riots at Pontarddulais and Efail-wen

There was a series of riots all across Britain in the 1830s. Some called for the Charter to be made law, and others happened because people were so poor or felt they were being treated unfairly. You can see memorials to some of these riots in Pembrokeshire and Carmarthenshire, and in the towns of Llanidloes, Powys, and Newport, Gwent, where the Chartists were very active. Hundreds of Chartists came from the works in the valleys to Newport in November 1839, and many were killed in a violent fight in the middle of the town.

Between 1839 and 1846 people in west Wales attacked the tollgates. There were a lot of those in that area, and the companies had some unfair ways of trying to get the tolls paid. So, men would dress up to look like women, to stop people recognising them, and then they would go out at night, attack the tollgates and destroy them.

There is a verse in the Bible which says Rebecca's children would possess the gates of those that hate them, and it is likely that this is why these riots were called the Rebecca Riots.

HISTORY GROUNDED

John Frost (1784-1877)

John Frost was born in Newport, but brought up in Bristol. He learnt to be a tailor, and set up in business in Newport in 1806. The business was successful, and he became an important man in the town. He was intelligent and energetic, and had very radical ideas. He was elected to the Town Council in 1835 and soon there was a disagreement between him and some other important men, especially Thomas Prothero, the town clerk, and Sir Charles Morgan, the richest and most important man in the area.

John Frost

Frost began to think that only when every man got the vote would it be possible to improve things. He was a strong supporter of the People's Charter, and he started to argue publicly for it.

It isn't surprising that he was chosen as their leader by the crowds of Chartists who were calling for an armed attack on the cruel and unjust authorities. The odd thing is that Frost himself argued against this. But the

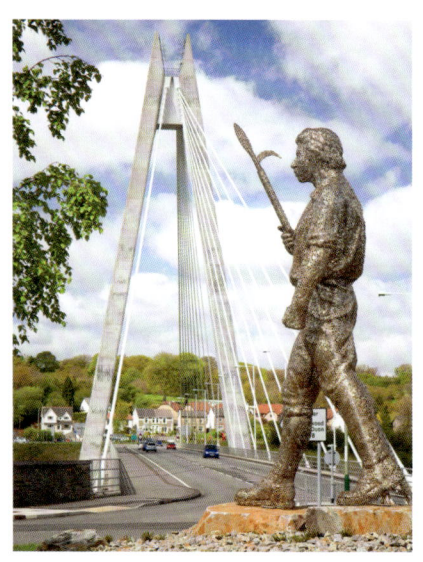

The Chartist Bridge and the Chartist statue at Blackwood

The memorial stone for the Chartists killed at Newport, and who were buried somewhere in the graveyard of St Woolos Cathedral in the city

HISTORY GROUNDED

A drawing of the Chartist marchers scattering as the soldiers fired on them from the Westgate Hotel, Newport

decision was still taken to attack Newport on 3 November 1839. Frost burst into tears when he heard this.

The attack failed and Frost was arrested. He went on trial in January 1840, and he and two of the other leaders were condemned to be executed for high treason: hanged, drawn and quartered. That was the last time that dreadful punishment was pronounced. There were protests against the sentence, and it was decided to send Frost and his friends to Australia forever.

But the campaign for Frost carried on, and in 1854 he was pardoned. He came back to live with his family in Bristol. To the end of his life he carried on arguing for the rights of man and for the need to give the vote to every man. Before he died he saw the vote granted to another million men by the Second Parliamentary Reform Act, 1867.

Frost was a villain in the eyes of most people after what happened in 1839. But, as the Chartist ideas became reality, people changed their opinion of him. There are several memorials to him now, and the central square in Newport is named after him, as well as one of the city's secondary schools.

Elizabeth Miles (1847-1930)

John Frost was a man who fought against the unfairness of his time. Elizabeth Miles was a woman who fought to make a living for herself and her children, and she made the most of every chance she got.

When her husband died in 1869, Elizabeth Miles was the mother of two tiny children. So, she had to find a way of keeping herself and her family. She began to run a little pub in the Rhondda, with the help of her niece and another young girl. This is the time when the Rhondda coal mines were developing quickly, and lots of young men were coming to the area looking for work – and somewhere to stay.

Elizabeth Miles

Before long Mrs Miles was running a bigger pub, and then another one, bigger still, with more and more people to help her. By 1886 she was running the biggest hotel in Pontypridd. She owned several other businesses in that town and others nearby.

In 1897 she saw another opportunity. It had become fashionable for people to go to the "spa towns" of Builth Wells, Llanwrtyd Wells and Llandrindod Wells. The word "wells" in these names reminds us how important the wells or springs of water were there. People believed that the water from these wells was good for their health. They would go there for holidays to "take the waters". There were several hotels in Llandrindod, and Mrs Miles decided to buy one of them.

When she bought the Bridge Hotel, it was a respectable hotel, which could take 40 guests. During the following years, Mrs Miles expanded the hotel until there was room there for 200 guests, and she changed its name to the Metropole. By 1923 it was the biggest hotel in Wales,

HISTORY GROUNDED

The Metropole Hotel, Llandrindod; an iron tap for the water from one of the springs in the town

and one of the most luxurious and modern too.

Mrs Miles retired to Pontypridd in 1925, and handed over the Metropole to her children. Their descendants still own the Metropole today. And there is a portrait of Mrs Miles in the entrance to the hotel, still welcoming visitors.

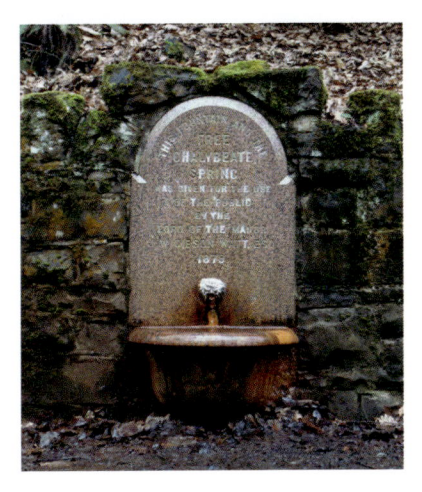

HISTORY GROUNDED

The railways in Wales by 1914

156

HISTORY GROUNDED

Almshouses at Llanrwst

Llanfyllin workhouse, which is a museum now. You can see what life was like for the people who had to live in the "poorhouse".

Improvements

But in spite of these riots, and perhaps because of them, things began to get better in the second half of the 19C. The government had begun to inquire into the working conditions in industry. Laws were passed to make things better. Employing children in coal mines and factories was banned. Every area had to look after poor people and those who needed care, and make sure that children were educated. Towns had to build sewage systems too and get a supply of clean water to houses. Some rich people began to think more about the welfare of their workers. They built schools for the children, almshouses for the elderly, and hospitals for the sick and for those injured at work. They would also join the committees which built the workhouses and hospitals for the mentally ill.

You can still see lots of the buildings from that time. Some look pretty, but some, especially the hospitals and workhouses for the poor, look more like prisons. Even though rich people were now more willing to help people who weren't as lucky as them, they didn't think they should enjoy themselves! From about 1850 onwards, people built with confidence, expecting their work to last for many years. This is the time of big, impressive buildings like the chapels and churches you can see in every town today, and in many villages too. Many of them are closed now, or have been turned into homes or businesses. Look for the dates on them that tell you when they were built.

A network of railways made it possible to travel quickly, safely and quite cheaply. The railways made it easier to take heavy goods to the big towns and the ports. In the second half of the 19C many towns in Wales were growing fast, and the houses were so good that some of them are still comfortable homes today, like the houses seen below in Bute Town, Rhymney, which were built in the 1830s, nearly 200 years ago.

These houses have slate roofs. The houses in the slate industry villages, from Rosebush, Pembrokeshire, to Bethesda, Gwynedd, look very alike and belong to the same period – like the houses below in Blaenau Ffestiniog, which belong to the rock and the mounds of the mountain.

Because of all the wealth and the building, the industrial buildings were big too, and they were solid, meant to last for hundreds of years. But that isn't what happened. By the beginning of the 20C oil and electricity were beginning to take the place of coal and steam, and there were other big changes just around the corner.

Capel Mawr, Tal-y-sarn, Dyffryn Nantlle, which has closed now

A row of well-built houses, with slate roofs, at Bute Town, Rhymney

The town of Blaenau Ffestiniog in the shadow of the slate tips

Ports

The port of Holyhead, Anglesey, was established by an Act of Parliament in 1845. By 1906 there was a ferry service between Fishguard and Ireland. Because so many people wanted to use the ferries, the ports of Pembroke Dock and Swansea started them too. By the beginning of the 21C, Holyhead had grown to be an important port on the route between Europe and Ireland.

The Irish mail steamships in Holyhead harbour, 1925

Ports and towns grew all along the coast of south-east Wales because of the growth of the coal trade. In 1881, only 85 people lived in Barry. Then, in 1889, David Davies the coal-owner opened a port there for the coal from his mines in the Rhondda. By 1913, Barry was the busiest coal exporting port in the world, and about 40,000 people lived there.

The statue of David Davies in Barry

HISTORY GROUNDED

A Bangor school – hundreds of schools like this one were built all over Wales in the second half of the 19C

Making Wales English

You will have noticed, perhaps, that the words on this memorial are in English, although most people spoke Welsh in this area at that time. English was the only official language in Wales since the time of Henry VIII, although most people in Wales could only speak Welsh then and for centuries afterwards. By the end of the 19C English was the language of education, the language of the law courts, the language of all the important things in the world.

Many people learnt to speak English, of course, but most Welsh people chose to go on speaking Welsh. Perhaps this was because it was possible to live and work without using English. But perhaps it was because they loved the language too, and connected it with home, not the world of work and business. The fact that religion was so important to them, and that they had the Bible in Welsh, strengthened that feeling. The services in

HISTORY GROUNDED

the Nonconformist chapels were in Welsh too in the areas where Welsh was spoken.

Between 1734 and 1779 many Welsh people had learnt to read and write Welsh by going to temporary schools set up by the Reverend Griffith Jones. But after that scheme ended, although there were schools available for people who wanted their children to be educated, the quality of these schools varied a lot. The teaching there was in English too, and parents could choose to send their children to school – or not.

Welsh Not – this was found under the floor of a Bangor school

A drawing to show how it might have felt to have to wear the Welsh Not

161

The Infants class in Pentreuchaf School, Llŷn, in 1926

But from 1870 on, every area had to elect a committee to set up a school for children from 5 to 12 years of age, if there wasn't a school in that area. There were lots of schools before then, set up by the church or chapels, or by rich people who thought children should be educated. From 1880 on every child between 5 and 10 had to go to school. All the lessons in these schools were in the official language of the country – English. In some schools children were punished for speaking Welsh.

Lots of the primary schools that were built in the 19C are still schools today, like this one, Ysgol Pentreuchaf, Pwllheli. They are easy to spot: one-storey buildings, with big windows high up (so the children couldn't look out, but concentrated on their lessons). At first there was only one big room in these schools. All the children would be taught together, and older children had to help the younger ones with their work.

Until 1851 nobody counted how many people spoke Welsh. So we don't know for certain when some Welsh people started to choose to speak English rather than Welsh. But by the middle of the 20C people began to worry that the language would die, and started to campaign to try to save it.

Vulcana (Miriam Kate Williams, 1874-1946)

By the end of the 19C the world was changing very quickly. One of these adventurous women was Miriam Kate Williams. She was the daughter of a preacher in Abergavenny, but she chose a very different way of life.

When she was 15, Kate started to attend a gymnasium for girls, which had just been opened in Abergavenny. She fell in love with the owner of the gymnasium, and the two ran away together, although he was older than her and already married. From then on they earned their living by giving displays of strength and fitness. This was in the time before the cinema, when popular theatres – the music halls – were in every town.

So Vulcana and Atlas were performers, and there was more than a bit of cheating in their performances. The weights they lifted weren't always as "heavy" as they said! But they were very popular, especially in France, and there is plenty of good evidence that Vulcana was amazingly strong.

HISTORY GROUNDED

A MYSTERY IN THE GROUND

Why wasn't the Severn Bridge built in 1845?

The Severn Bridge, 1966

The first bridge to cross the Severn Estuary was opened in 1966. But detailed plans for such a bridge had been published in 1845 by a man from Nant-y-glo, Gwent. Samuel Baldwyn Rogers was a scientist and an amazing inventor. He invented a new method of making iron which proved very popular. He wrote a standard textbook on metallurgy which was used for years, and he was full of practical, new ideas.

Many of Samuel Rogers's ideas were used, but most of them years after he died in 1863. He wanted to start a school for miners in south Wales: a school like that was opened in Trefforest, Pontypridd, in 1913. He suggested setting up a fund to help miners who had been injured at work: a fund like that was set up in 1919. And in 1966 a bridge across the Severn Estuary was opened, in the exact place Samuel Rogers had suggested.

Samuel Baldwyn Rogers

Rogers did not live to see his dreams come true, and he did not benefit from all his technological improvements. His contribution was acknowledged after he died a poor man following a long illness. His greatest fear on his death bed was that he would be given a pauper's burial. Through the kindness of friends his remains were put to rest in the same grave as his wife, an unmarked grave in the graveyard of the small church of Llanfoist, near Abergavenny. The last of his children died in a workhouse in Newport.

The usual description of a succesful innovator is 'a man before his time'. But it is possible to be too progressive, going too far ahead of your time – and that is what happened to Samuel Baldwyn Rogers.

HISTORY GROUNDED

World War I 1914-1918
World War II 1939-1945

The National Health Service 1946

The capital city of Wales 195...

Dates

Part 4: Timeline

Questions

- What was so new about memorials for the soldiers of the First World War?
- How did Wales help to make the National Health Service?

HISTORY GROUNDED

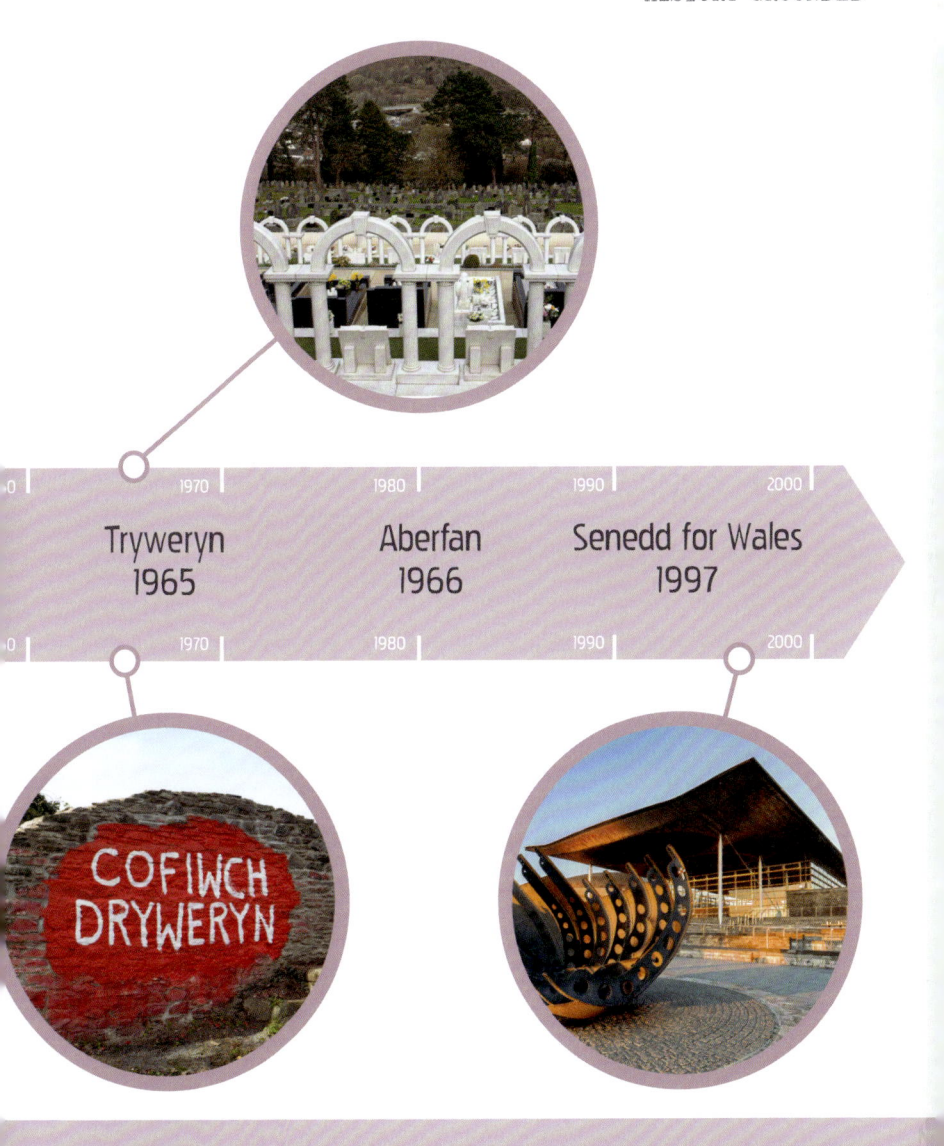

| Tryweryn | Aberfan | Senedd for Wales |
| 1965 | 1966 | 1997 |

- Which city is the newest capital city in Europe?
- Why is water such a burning issue in Wales?
- What happened at Aberfan?
- How long did it take for Wales to have a Senedd again?

167

HISTORY GROUNDED

The century of ordinary people

By 1900 life had got better for lots of people in Wales, but some of them still felt that things weren't fair for some people. Workers didn't get much pay, even though the owners of the industries and the landowners were making lots of money. Many houses were still in poor condition, and many people, including children, were living on the streets. Rich people were still building huge, grand houses, with lots of servants to look after them. Although most of the demands of the People's Charter had been met, only 60% of men had the vote, and no women could vote at all.

Britain had a new Chancellor of the Exchequer in 1908, and he had some new ideas. His name was David Lloyd George. He was a Welshman and wanted to make life better for poor people in Britain. The Chancellor is the person who decides how to spend the money that the Government gets from taxes. Lloyd George and his supporters in Parliament began to change how this money was spent. Some of the money from taxes now started to go towards paying for pensions for old people and giving some income to people who couldn't work because they were ill. Poor people across Britain praised Lloyd George, and he was a hero to people in Wales!

Lloyd George became an even bigger hero a few years later, when Britain went to war with Germany. This was the beginning of the First World War, and things did not go well for Britain to begin with. Then, in 1916, Lloyd George became Prime Minister of Britain, and by the end of 1918 Germany and Britain had made peace.

Lloyd George wanted to thank ordinary people for working so hard for their country during the war. In 1918 a law was passed which gave the vote to every man over 21 and to women too – if they were over 30.

HISTORY GROUNDED

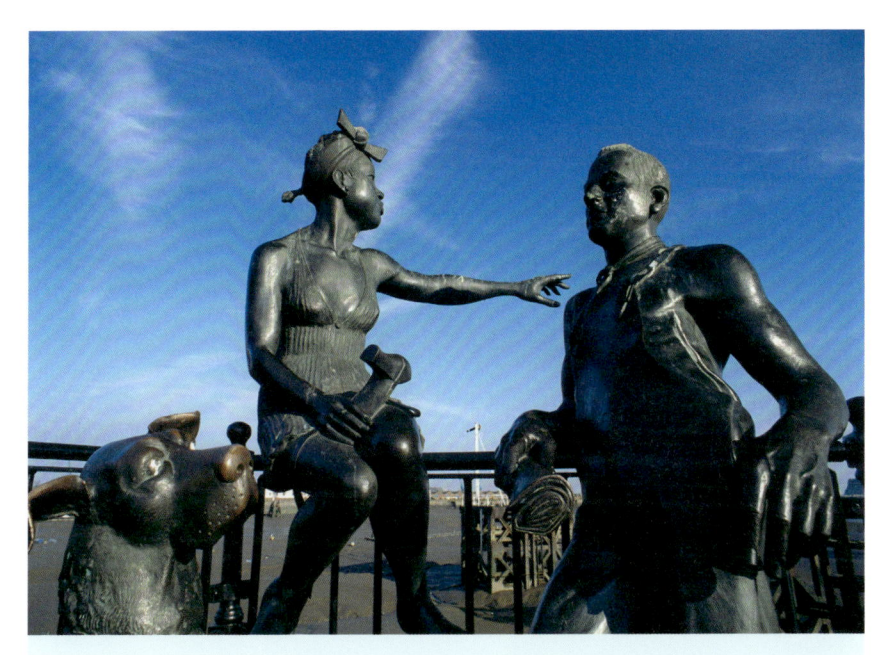

A modern memorial celebrating the lives of the people of Tiger Bay, in what used to be Cardiff docks. The area is now called Cardiff Bay. The name of the statue says it all: 'People Like Us'.

It would take another ten years before women had the vote on the same terms as men.

Memorials

There are several statues of Lloyd George – one near the Houses of Parliament in London, one in Caernarfon (he was the Member of Parliament for Caernarfon), and one in the centre of Cardiff. That was what people used to do in those days – put up statues in honour of famous people. You will see lots of them all around the country. They have two things in common: (1) they are all white men: there are no statues like this of women, even white ones; (2) most people have forgotten those men who were so important in their time.

The confident people of the 19C liked to put up statues like these in honour of their heroes. Many of them had become famous because they were soldiers, others just because they were rich, or because they had done important jobs.

HISTORY GROUNDED

The national memorial to those who died in the two World Wars, Cathays Park, Cardiff

Some war memorials in Wales are only in Welsh, and some of them don't use words like 'honour' and 'heroes' either, but call the soldiers who were killed 'bechgyn' ('boys') or 'hogiau' ('lads'). The memorial to Hedd Wyn, the poet from Trawsfynydd who was killed in the First World War, shows him as a shepherd, not a soldier.

But at the end of the First World War something new happened. Thousands upon thousands of young men had been killed in the war, and it was decided that memorials should be put up for them. For the first time, ordinary people were honoured with official memorials. There is a war memorial in almost every British town and village, and on them are the names of those killed in the fighting. Sometimes the memorial lists them according to their rank in the armed forces, but sometimes, as on this memorial (above, right) this isn't mentioned. Today, we think that the lives of ordinary people should be remembered in statues and memorials.

The law-abiding suffragists of Cardiff with their banner

Votes for Women!

Although women over 30 got the right to vote in 1918, some women had been campaigning for this for years. Rose Mary Crawshay held a meeting in Merthyr Tudful in 1866 to organise a petition to Parliament to ask for women to have the vote. That petition was refused, and the same thing happened to the other petitions that were organised during the next fifty years.

But the movement was growing, and in 1913 a huge rally was held in London to call for the vote. Women from all parts of Wales marched to this rally. They emphasised the fact that they wanted to gain the vote by peaceful and law-abiding methods. That was because a new movement had been started in 1908 which asked women to do violent and shocking things to draw attention to their cause. These women were called suffragettes.

Branches of this new movement were started in Wales too – the Cardiff branch as early as 1908. Their violent protests certainly got them noticed. The suffragettes would break windows, set letter boxes on fire, and shout out in public meetings like the National Eisteddfod – and even during Lloyd George's speeches!

Women didn't get the vote on exactly the same terms as men until 1928. Only some women over 30 had the vote in 1918, and there were conditions even to their rights.

HISTORY GROUNDED

A charabanc at the foot of Rhiw hill, Llŷn

A changing world

As the 20C went on, new kinds of fuel like oil and electricity became more popular. This wasn't a good thing for some Welsh industries, and they suffered because of this. At the same time, it was easy to import food from countries a long way away, so farming suffered too. The 1920s and 1930s were very hard years. Many people went to England to look for work, or further away, to the USA, Canada or Australia.

A row of Ford cars in Ceredigion; an early garage in Denbigh town

But in these years new things arrived which made life easier for those who could afford them. This is the time when the motor car became popular, and you can still see some of the first garages built in Wales.

Buses became popular too. People who could afford it went on holiday to the seaside, and on trips in big open cars, the *charabancs*.

And this is the time the cinema became popular. Some of the early ones have been closed or turned into bingo halls or pubs, but you can still see the buildings in some places.

The Second World War

Although people thought at the time that the First World War would be the last worldwide war ever, that isn't what happened. The countries of Europe went to war again in 1939, and when they made peace again in 1945, other changes had happened to the world and to Wales too.

The old Market Hall cinema in Bryn-mawr, which has been repaired to show how it used to look

One of them was the destruction made by bombing from the air. Thousands of people were killed, and homes, factories, roads, bridges and railways were destroyed. A large part of the middle of Swansea disappeared in three nights of bombing in 1941, and 230 people were killed.

A photograph showing bomb damage in the middle of Swansea

But other communities were destroyed too – in a different way. The army took over parts of the country in order to train soldiers for the war. The most famous of these areas in Wales is Mynydd Epynt. A total of 219 people were moved out of their farms in 1939, and the whole area is still being used by the army. Nobody lives there now.

The government was afraid the enemy would invade Britain from the sea. So, huge rolls of barbed wire were put over the beaches and enormous blocks of concrete too. These have disappeared by now, although you can still see a block or two of concrete in some places. Buildings were made for guns too, and there are still lots of these to be seen.

A red warning flag near an old farmhouse on Mynydd Epynt. The ruined farm is only a number now.

Tanks still practise at Castlemartin, Pembrokeshire

A row of concrete blocks – sea defences – you can still see at the mouth of the Mawddach, Meirionnydd

This gun shelter is above the harbour at Aberystwyth

The Welfare State

When peace was announced in 1945, people wanted to see life getting better. Plans had been made during the war to improve schools and to carry on with Lloyd George's work by looking after the old, the poor and the vulnerable. Lots of the houses built in the 19C were cleared away. They had become slums. The people who had lived in them were moved to new houses with all the modern things – bathrooms and indoor toilets. These houses look old-fashioned to us today, but everyone admired them at the time!

A modern kitchen in a 'Plan your home' exhibition for the new houses that were being built after the Second World War

But the biggest change was inventing a way to make sure that every single person in the country had health care absolutely free. This was the beginning of the National Health Service. Before that, you had to pay a doctor to look after you. Oddly enough, when you remember what Lloyd George did, it was another Welshman, called Aneurin Bevan, who was responsible for setting up the National Health Service.

Cardiff houses destroyed by the bombs of the Second World War, January 1941

Aneurin Bevan (1897-1960)

Aneurin Bevan was the son of a miner from Tredegar, Gwent. He didn't like school, and went to work in the pit with his father when he was 13. He saw how poor the area was and how unfairly the workmen were treated by the companies which owned the pits. He was interested in politics, and believed that it was only by using their vote that people could make their lives better.

He became a member of the Labour Party and the local council in 1928, and MP for Ebbw Vale in 1929. He had lots of energy, was very determined and could make good speeches. He wanted to speak in public, although he had a stammer. So, he taught himself to talk better by walking the hills above Tredegar, shouting his speeches into the wind. He was very clever too, and ready to fight for what he thought was right. Before long he became well known for his fiery speeches and his gift for saying clever, hurtful things.

The old cemetery at Cefn Golau in Blaenau Gwent reminds us how poor health care was once. This is where people who died of cholera had to be buried – a long way from anywhere. But the Aneurin Bevan hospital (above) at Ebbw Vale today reminds us of the politician who started the Health Service to help everyone.

HISTORY GROUNDED

He became Minister for Health in 1945, and began setting up a national service which would be like the Tredegar Medical Aid Society. A lot of people were against his plans, but Aneurin Bevan had the energy and the ability to defeat this. Remembering his father's cruel death in 1925 inspired him too. His father had died as a result of breathing in the dust underground.

But Aneurin Bevan was a fighter, and he loved conflict and fierce argument. In 1948 he described people who were against him as "lower than vermin". Before long he had quarrelled with the leaders of his own party. He wasn't given any important work after 1951, and he died in 1960.

But Welsh people still remember him. There is a statue of him in the middle of Cardiff, and streets are named after him too. In an opinion poll in 2004, Aneurin Bevan was chosen as Wales' greatest hero.

A statue of Aneurin Bevan in one of the main streets in Cardiff

The offices of the Tredegar Medical Aid Society today

HISTORY GROUNDED

Pulling down a chapel in the old village of Llanwddyn to create a reservoir; one of the dams in Cwm Elan

Tryweryn

There are lots of lakes in Wales, and although some of them, like Lake Tegid, near Bala, are natural lakes, many of them are artificial. They are reservoirs for towns nearby. A lot of them were made in the 19C, as towns and industries grew.

Some of these lakes were made for towns in the west of England, like Birmingham and Manchester. Llyn Efyrnwy, Powys, which was finished in 1889, was made for the city of Liverpool. Although these artificial lakes were in country areas, farms and, sometimes, whole villages had to be drowned in order to make them. The village of Llanwddyn was drowned by the water of Llyn Efyrnwy.

There wasn't much opposition to this at the time. Perhaps that was because ordinary people didn't have much of a say in decisions like these. A city would ask Parliament for permission to build the reservoir it needed, and Parliament would give permission. Very few people lived in the Welsh countryside compared to the thousands that lived in the English cities.

But when the city of Liverpool asked for permission to build another reservoir in Wales in 1960, in the area of Tryweryn, Gwynedd, this time, things had changed. By now, everyone over 21 had a vote, and a lot of Welsh people didn't want to see another Welsh village drowned. There were big protests against Liverpool's request. When it was discussed

HISTORY GROUNDED

The people of Cwm Tryweryn asking for help in the streets of Liverpool (left); the children of Capel Celyn before their school was closed and pulled down (right)

in Parliament, 35 out of the 36 MPs from Wales voted against giving permission. But there were 594 members of Parliament. The vote was lost, and Liverpool City Council was given permission to make Llyn Celyn in Tryweryn.

The protests went on, and two men were sent to prison for placing explosives at the site. The people of Capel Celyn community had to be forced to leave their homes, and all of this was seen on television. From now on, more and more people in Wales were asking for independence. The words "Cofiwch Dryweryn" ("Remember Tryweryn"), painted on a wall by the road between Aberystwyth and Aberaeron, have become a popular slogan in Wales recently.

The original writing on the ruined cottage at Llanrhystud has been restored. One of many copies of it on a van in Penrhyndeudraeth in 2019

HISTORY GROUNDED

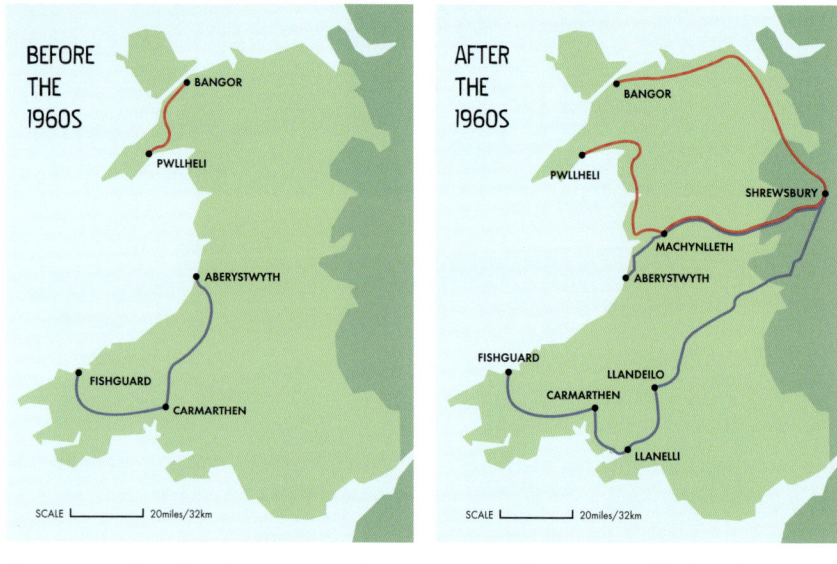

Two maps showing the same two journeys – one between Pwllheli and Bangor, and one between Aberystwyth and Fishguard – before and after so many railway lines in Wales were closed in the 1960s

Factories and motorways

There were lots of changes in the 1960s, in work, travel, fashion and music.

New factories were built instead of the old coal mines, slate quarries and iron furnaces. Because more and more machines were being used on farms, fewer people were need for farm work. More and more people could afford to go abroad for their holidays, and to buy a car too, while lorries were being used to carry goods.

The railways had linked many seaside places with big towns. So, holidays by the sea had been very popular. But that changed in the 1960s too. Some small railway lines had been closed before the Second World War. But in the 1960s 6,000 miles of railway were closed out of the total of 18,000 miles there had been altogether across Britain. Lots of the small country railways closed, like the line between Whitland and Cardigan, the "Cardi Bach" railway. And now the lines built for the heavy industries weren't needed any longer. Lots of them have been turned into

HISTORY GROUNDED

One of the engines which ran on the Cardi Bach line in Cardigan station before the tracks were taken away.

footpaths and cycle tracks now.

Although people looked back longingly at the old ways of living, working and travelling, young people felt very much that the world belonged to them, and not their parents. They welcomed the

The Berlei factory in Ebbw Vale in 1951

new fashions, the pop music, the jobs in offices and factories which were clean, safe – and brand new. They also believed that the world could be changed by asking people to love one another and turn their backs on war and violence.

HISTORY GROUNDED

Two of Wales' busiest roads: (above, left) the Britannia bridge on the A55 to Chester; (above, right) the M4 from south Wales to London

A missing motorway?

One look at a map of motorways in Wales shows you that the two important motorways are the A55 along the coast of north Wales, and the M4 in the south. These roads were built to connect the ferry ports of Wales with the big towns in England. There aren't many other good roads in Wales. In 1979 the A470 was marked as the link road of 186 miles/299 km between Llandudno and Cardiff. But there are lot of difficult stretches on it, and it still goes through the middle of some towns and villages.

Some of the tight corners on the A470 in Llanrwst and on Pont-yr-Afanc, near Betws-y-coed

HISTORY GROUNDED

Wales and the Peace Movement

The war memorials of the 20C and the pictures of the bomb damage in the Second World War show us that war and fighting have been part of the lives of Welsh people until very recently.

Many Welsh people were very willing to take part in these wars, and many were forced into them too. We have to admire the bravery and the comradeship of soldiers, while hating the effect of war on families and communities. But during the last century people have campaigned against war, and many Welsh people have been part of this campaign.

There is a statue in Tregaron of one of the first of these campaigners: Henry Richard MP (1812–1888). He campaigned against slavery too, and he became called "The Apostle of Peace". Many of the statues of the Victorian Age celebrate soldiers, but here is one to a peace campaigner.

Gwilym Davies, another minister, worked hard after the First World War to get people to see how wasteful and cruel war is. In 1922, he started the annual peace message from the children of Wales to the world. The Urdd organises this today, and perhaps you've taken part in it.

In the 20C women have taken part in peace campaigns as well. In 1923, after the First World War, the women of Wales organised a huge Peace Petition with 390,396 names on it.

Protests were seen in Wales when the government in London took

Henry Richard's statue in Tregaron

possession of land for military uses. An RAF Bombing School in Llŷn suffered an arson attack in 1936 and vocal protests against further land seizure were seen in the Preseli hills (1946) and Trawsfynydd (1951). Nuclear bombs were used on Japan at the end of the Second World War and people have campaigned against nuclear weapons ever since.

In 1981 a group of women from Wales walked to Greenham Common in the south of England. They set up a peace camp at Greenham, around the huge store of nuclear weapons there. They tried to stop the army vehicles going in and out of the camp. Hundreds of them were arrested, and some were sent to prison. One of them Helen Wyn Thomas from Newcastle Emlyn – was killed in a collision with a police vehicle.

There was a peace camp at Greenham for 19 years, and the nuclear weapons were taken from there in the end. There is a memorial garden there now, which has a circle of stones from Wales in memory of Helen Wyn Thomas.

A bench placed in memory of Helen Thomas in her birthplace, Newcastle Emlyn, in 2011

HISTORY GROUNDED

A memorial to the three activists who set fire to the Bombing School at Penyberth, Llŷn, in 1936

A strong protest to prevent the army taking possession of more land at Trawsfynydd in 1951

HISTORY GROUNDED

Senedd i Gymru? A Parliament for Wales?

For 200 years ordinary people had been asking for the vote to give them more of a voice in the way the country was being run. The Chartists were asking for the vote in 1839 and the suffragettes in 1908. In the second half of the 19C the people of Wales, Scotland and Ireland began to ask for the right to decide some things for themselves too, instead of all the decisions being made a long way away in London.

The disappointment over Tryweryn and other things, like forcing the farmers to leave their farms on Mynydd Epynt, made people think that the Parliament in London wasn't ready to pay attention to the problems of Wales. A Minister for Welsh Affairs was appointed in 1951 though – someone who would speak for Wales in Parliament.

In 1955 Megan Lloyd George, a Member of Parliament and the daughter of Lloyd George, began a campaign for a parliament for Wales. The Parliament in London began to make more changes. But before long these weren't enough. In 1966 Gwynfor Evans of Plaid Cymru was elected as Member of Parliament for Carmarthen. Plaid Cymru's aim was to have a Parliament for Wales, but although the party had been set up in 1925, it had never won a parliamentary election

The Campaign for a Parliament for Wales in the 1950s – a publicity stall by Plaid Cymru, with harpist Nansi Richards, at Llanrhaeadr-ym-Mochnant, May 1957

HISTORY GROUNDED

Gwynfor Evans on the morning after he was elected as Plaid Cymru's first MP

before. There were more protests and more campaigning in the 1960s and 1970s.

In the end, Wales was given the chance to have its say about getting its own Parliament. A referendum was held in 1997. A referendum is the voice of the people, and usually only one question is asked, with one simple answer: Yes or No. In 1997 the people of Wales were asked if they wanted a Parliament. The answer was 'Yes' – but only just! This result was positively confirmed in a 2011 referendum by a 4:1 majority.

The new Senedd (*'parliament'*) which was opened in Cardiff in 1999 only had limited powers. It could make decisions about education, health, the environment and the care of children and old people. But it has more powers today.

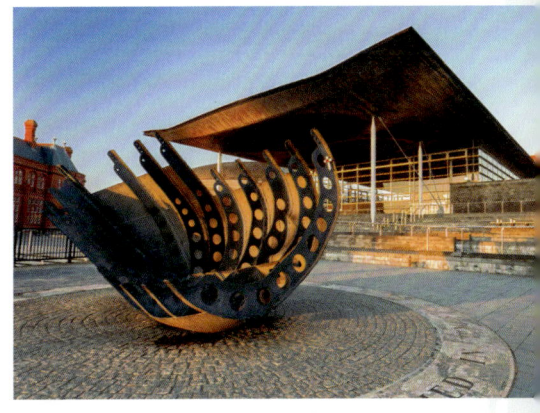

The Senedd building in Cardiff Bay

It has made decisions to limit smoking and the use of plastic. It has set up a Commissioner to look after children's welfare, created the Welsh Coastal Path, and is working to get more people to recycle and to speak Welsh.

HISTORY GROUNDED

There's always something new to do at the Urdd camp in Llangrannog

Urdd Gobaith Cymru

Joining Urdd Gobaith Cymru has helped many children to enjoy themselves in Welsh. This youth movement has had a lot of influence in every part of the country over the last hundred years. It was started by Ifan ab Owen Edwards in 1922 with the aim of offering fun activities in Welsh for children and young people.

The Urdd is the biggest youth movement in Wales today, with over 55,000 members. It has centres in Cardiff Bay, Llanuwchllyn and Llangrannog. As well as the activities organised in its centres and a range of different sports events, the Urdd National Eisteddfod is held in a different place in Wales every year. In 1976 the movement's badge became a cute, lively cartoon character – are *you* one of Mr Urdd's friends?

The founder, Ifan ab Owen Edwards

The first Urdd branch throughout Wales was set up at Treuddyn, a Flintshire village on Offa's Dyke Path.

HISTORY GROUNDED

One of the first classes at Ysgol Dewi Sant, Llanelli

Education and the Welsh Language

Ysgol Dewi Sant in Llanelli was opened in 1947. This was the first local authority primary school to teach entirely in Welsh. Other primary schools like it were opened in the years that followed. The first Welsh-language secondary school, Ysgol Glan Clwyd, was opened in Rhyl in 1956. These schools became very popular.

Today, there are many primary and secondary schools teaching in Welsh today. Every school pupil has to learn Welsh as a subject in secondary school too. But there wasn't much opportunity to do university courses in Welsh. In 2011 the Coleg Cymraeg was started, to provide teaching in the Welsh in the universities of Wales.

Norah Isaac, the headteacher of Ysgol Lluest, Aberystwyth – an independent Welsh school started by Urdd Gobaith Cymru in 1939

HISTORY GROUNDED

Eileen Beasley (1921-2012)

Usually, it's young people who take part in protests, and there were lots of young people in the protests of the 1960s. Young singers became famous for their protest songs in the United States of America and here in Wales too. Dafydd Iwan, the most famous of the Welsh protest singers, could draw hundreds of people to villages halls all across Wales to hear his inspiring songs.

But other people supported the young protesters. Some of them were people no one would have expected to see taking part in any sort of protest. Eileen Beasley was one of these. She was a teacher and the mother of a young family when she and her husband, Trefor, decided to ask Llanelli Borough Council to have their bills in Welsh. The Council refused, and Eileen and Trefor decided not to pay the money.

Eileen Beasley and her two children in the shadow of the English-only tax demand

The plaque on the Beasleys' old home in Llangennech

Eileen and Trefor's campaign went on for ten years. They had to go to court 16 times because they were refusing to pay the money they owed the Council. People from the Council came to their house to take away some of their furniture to pay off the debt. Trefor had to go to prison. Some people in their village wouldn't speak to them. When Eileen went to fetch her children from school, some of the other parents would turn their backs on her.

But in 1960 the Council gave in, and Eileen and Trefor had a bill in Welsh and English. In 2015 Llanelli Council arranged for a blue plaque to be put on the family's old home – and today every official form that comes from a local council or the central government is in Welsh and English.

The tragedy of Aberfan

For years you could see the tips – the waste heaps from the coal mines – on top of the hills in every valley in the coal-mining areas of Wales. You would still see them there today probably, if a dreadful thing hadn't happened in Cwm Taf on 21 October 1966.

The children of the village of Aberfan had gone to their primary school as usual that

The path of the tip that destroyed the school and some of the houses in the village

morning: by dinner time 116 of them were dead, and 28 of the adults of the village too. They had all been killed by a flood of waste from a coal tip. The tip on the hill above the village had been built over a spring of water and heavy rain had undermined the whole tip. In minutes, this black slurry flowed down the hill and into the school. The children and their teachers could do nothing to protect themselves.

Losing so many little children in such a dreadful way touched the hearts of people all around the world. The dangers of what was left of the old heavy industries were obvious to everyone now. Work to clear the coal tips began straightaway after that, although people argued for years over who should pay for this work. The graves of the children are in the graveyard near the village, and the new woods growing on the valley hills are their memorial too.

The graves of the children at Aberfan

HISTORY GROUNDED

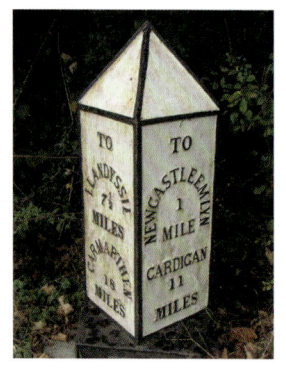

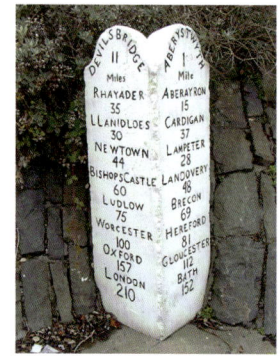

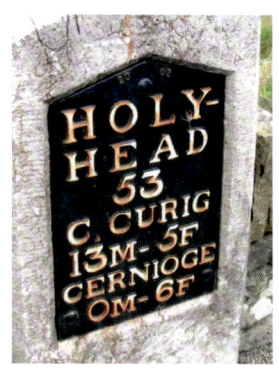

When people began to make maps of Wales and to build main roads with milestones on them, only the English names of the towns were used – and even the Welsh names were spelled the English way. But people kept on using the Welsh names.

Welsh Language Society (Cymdeithas yr Iaith)

From the beginning, one of Plaid Cymru's ideas was that Welsh should be as important in Wales as English. There was a lot of opposition to this idea though, as Eileen and Trefor Beasley had found. So, people began to challenge the authorities by insisting on using Welsh when they filled in official forms and things like that, and young people sang protest songs in Welsh. In 1962 Cymdeithas yr Iaith was formed to lead the campaign for the Welsh language.

You can see road signs in Welsh and English everywhere in Wales today, but for centuries every road sign was in English only. You would only see the English place names on signs in Wales. Although Welsh people would talk about going from *Caerfyrddin* to *Abertawe*, they would have to look for signs saying Swansea or Carmarthen.

Members of Cymdeithas yr Iaith began to go out at night to pull down the English-only road signs, or to paint over them. Many of them went to prison for doing this, but the protests went on.

It is very hard for a government to resist this sort of popular protest. So the British Government began to give the Welsh language more importance. You see bilingual signs everywhere now, and a lot of official notices in Welsh. The Senedd has passed more laws to protect the language.

HISTORY GROUNDED

The first protest by members of Cymdeithas yr Iaith on Trefechan bridge at Aberystwyth in 1963 (above) and Tedi Millward, one of the founding members of Cymdeithas yr Iaith, at a 50th anniversary of the original rally (right)

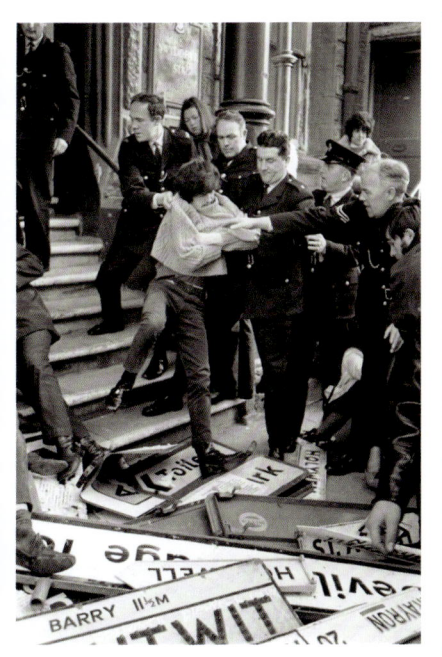

Policing one of Cymdeithas yr Iaith's protests against English-only road signs

A rally in Lampeter asking for Welsh to have equal status with English

HISTORY GROUNDED

An early view of Cardiff from Llandaf, looking down towards the docks and the Severn estuary (above); a photograph of Cardiff today (below), looking from the Bay towards the city centre. When you compare the two, you can see how the city has grown. It has swallowed up the little villages that were not part of the city in the past – villages like Rhiwbina, Llanedyrn, Ely, Rhymney, Whitchurch and Fairwater.

HISTORY GROUNDED

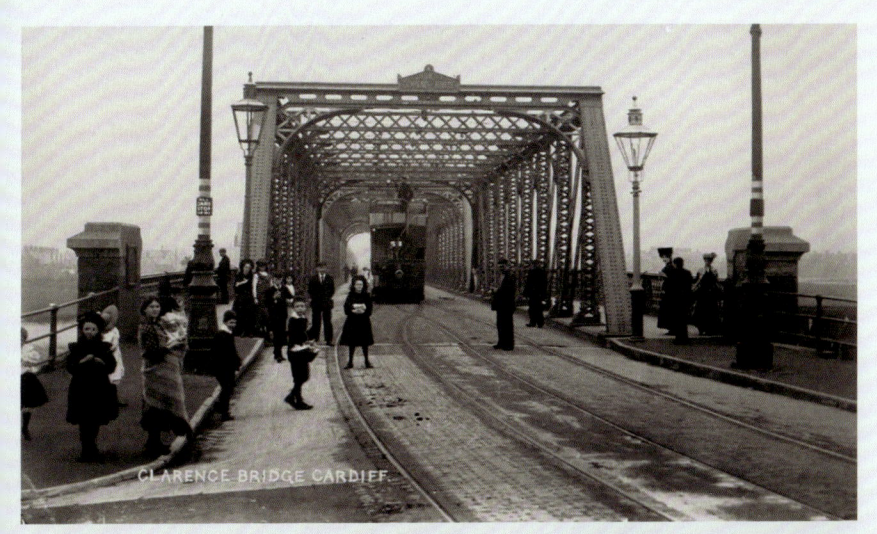

A tram crossing the Clarence bridge in the middle of Cardiff at the beginning of the 20C.

Cardiff becomes a capital city

The city grew from being a small, unimportant town to be the most important business centre in Wales, mainly because of the industries in the valleys. A total of 350,000 people live in Cardiff now – but two hundred years ago the population was only a few thousand: 1,870 in 1801. It is now an important location for international sports events and concerts and so on.

The National Museum of Wales

At the beginning of the 20C, as people felt more and more proud of their country and confident in the future, very grand buildings were built in Cathays Park – the university buildings, City Hall, the Law Courts and the National Museum. More recently, since the 1980s, the Millennium Centre, shops, restaurants and other attractions have been built in Cardiff Bay.

Cardiff is the newest capital city in Europe. It was given the status of a city in 1905, and became the capital city of Wales in October 1955.

HISTORY GROUNDED

A family cycling on the towpath of the Brecon and Monmouth Canal

WALES TODAY

Transport

You can walk along some of the old canals today, although some of them have vanished entirely. You can follow footpaths along some of the old railways that spread across Wales in the 19C, but which vanished in the 1960s.

One of the enormous tankers that use the deep water of the port of Haverfordwest

There aren't any toll gates at all in Wales now, and the busy roads that carry the traffic are all paid for out of taxes. There is more and more traffic on the roads. So, they have to be repaired regularly, and new roads and bridges built as well.

The little ports that were so busy for centuries are holiday villages now. The lime kilns are becoming ruins. Pleasure boats, not cargo ships, are at anchor in the harbour. Others, like Holyhead and Milford Haven, have expanded and are large, modern ports today.

HISTORY GROUNDED

There are lots of museums all across Wales on the sites of old works. You can experience something of those old industries there. Here are the Rhondda Heritage Park, Trehafod, and the Welsh Slate Museum, Llanberis (right). But a green energy revolution is starting now. Here are the wind turbines on Mynydd Gorddu, Ceredigion, below – and the sheep still grazing on the hills.

Industry

What there still is of the old industries of Wales is either in ruin or in museums. Although there are new industries here, they aren't in the middle of villages and towns. You have to wander near the big ports like Haverfordwest or through the enormous factory estates on the edge of towns if you want to see these industries. But usually, you aren't allowed to get near, because safety is much more important today than it was a century or more ago. One day these industries will vanish too, and people will look for their remains!

HISTORY GROUNDED

A group of men from local farms who have come to Rosa Bach farm, Prion, Denbigh, to help with the threshing, about 1910

Farming and Natural Resources Wales

There were lots of changes to farming in Wales during the 20C. Machines began to be used more, especially during the Second World War. Fewer people worked on the land. Because of the type of soil and because there is so much rain in Wales, growing grass for dairy and beef cows is the best way of farming here. In the past, whole families could live on the hill farms of Wales with the help of grants, but the future is uncertain. Farming methods over the centuries have shaped the countryside of Wales and created the beautiful landscapes you can see today. But some of the 20C's intensive farming methods have led to banks and hedges being destroyed, drying out wetlands that were important for wildlife, and endangering lots of species of birds, mammals and fish. Conservation bodies like the National Parks, the

HISTORY GROUNDED

Combine machines harvesting the corn in a field on Llŷn at the beginning of the 21 C

Areas of Outstanding Natural Beauty, and the government departments are working with farmers. They are trying to make sure that the valuable variety of wildlife is safeguarded, but that the demand for Welsh cheese, meat and other products is also met.

Cardigan Wildlife Park

Hafod Eryri at the top of Snowdon

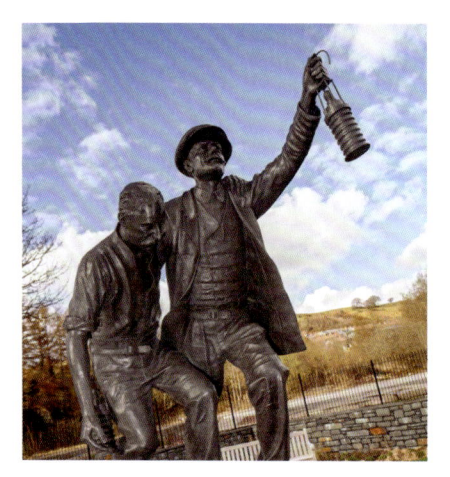

Part of the memorial at Senghennydd showing one of the brave men who went underground into the fire and danger to try to rescue some of the miners (left); the statue of Dic Evans, Moelfre (right)

Today's memorials

Two hundred years ago it was the fashion to put up memorials like statues to famous men, and you can see memorials like that everywhere in Wales. A hundred years ago, memorials started to be put up to ordinary people, like the soldiers who died in the First World War. It took another hundred years before we began to put up memorials to ordinary people who died because their work was so dangerous. The war memorial in Senghennydd was put up in 1921; in 2013 a memorial garden was opened there for all the miners who were killed at work. 152 disasters are listed there. The garden was opened exactly a century after 440 men were killed in one explosion in the colliery at Senghennydd.

Now, all across Wales there are statues and other memorials to remember the lives of ordinary people, and their part in the history of Wales. Dic Evans of Moelfre was a hero in many storms. He was the coxswain of the local lifeboat and steered the boat to save many lives when ships had got into difficulties on the east shore of Anglesey.

Plaques are put on buildings too because someone important lived there, or something important happened there – which is what happened with Eileen Beasley's old home.

HISTORY GROUNDED

Betty Campbell (1934-2017)

Very few of these memorials celebrate women's contribution to the history of Wales. But one of the latest memorials to be put up celebrates the work of one remarkable woman. Elizabeth (Betty) Campbell was a teacher, and she became the headteacher of Mount Stuart Primary School in Cardiff. She was black, like many of the children in her school. She had wanted to be a teacher ever since she was a child. But it was difficult for her — just because of the colour of her skin. She had done well in all her exams. In the end she managed to get a place at college and she began teaching at Mount Stuart School in 1970.

She was determined that the pupils of Mount Stuart School would know all their rich history. She would hold eisteddfodau at the school, and celebrated other religious and cultural festivals too. Her school became famous for its work, and Betty had lots of praise and attention for her vision and her tireless efforts on behalf of her community.

When it was decided that there needed to be a statue in the new Central Square in Cardiff, there were calls for a statue of a woman. Everyone agreed that, and then the woman had to be chosen. The BBC held a competition, and Betty Campbell was chosen.

Entertainment

The smart phones in our pockets can give us all sorts of films and music, and do it 24/7. But people still go to concerts and plays. Modern buildings like Pontio in Bangor, Theatr Clwyd in Mold and the Millennium Centre in Cardiff all offer a varied programme.

Pontio Arts Centre, Bangor

But some of the old 19C buildings are still open too. The Grand Theatre in Swansea was opened in 1897, and the New Theatre in Cardiff in 1907. They have been brought up to date, but they still look very much like they did a century ago.

Many of the performances in these centres are in English. If you want to have entertainment in Welsh, you will get that on S4C on television, and Radio Cymru 1 and 2. National Theatre Wales, which was started in 2003, travels round Wales with performances in Welsh and English.

Rugby is the symbol of Wales to many people, but people have been playing ball games here for a very long time. A book written in the 9C mentions boys playing ball games. The game called *cnapan* was a traditional sport in Pembrokeshire. Teams of young men would compete with each other for a ball, and there weren't many rules or

The Millennium Centre in Cardiff

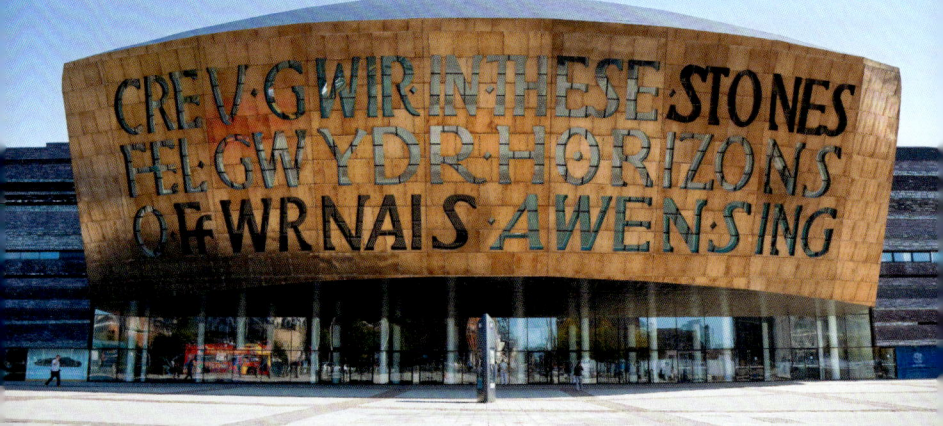

HISTORY GROUNDED

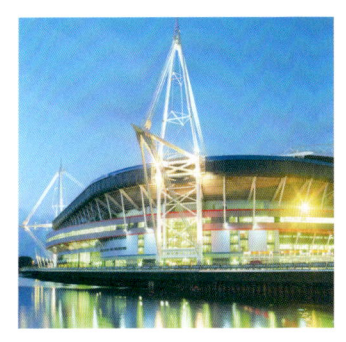

The national stadium in Cardiff

The national football team in the Euros in 2016

much organisation. Only in 1850 did men start to play rugby in Lampeter college, and that was probably the end of playing cnapan.

Bando, a game very like hockey, was played in south Wales in the 19C too. Once again, there weren't many rules, and lots of injuries. When people in Glamorgan want to say in Welsh that someone does things with all their strength, they say they are doing them *"braich a bando"* – "with their arm and their *bando* stick".

All these games are played on open fields, and you can't see anything today to show where those fields were. Later stands were built so that people could sit down to watch the game, and by today the Principality Stadium in Cardiff and the Liberty Stadium in Swansea can welcome thousands to watch the games there.

The hand ball court, Nelson, Caerphilly

Only three walls and a ball were needed to be able to play one very popular game – hand ball or fives. The players would hit the ball against the wall, and although ball courts were built specially for the game in some villages and schools, the game was played wherever there were suitable walls. Once again, there is nothing for us to see today, although one ball court is still standing in the village of Nelson, near Caerphilly.

But today, all sorts of games and adventure pursuits are part of the attractions of Wales for visitors.

HISTORY GROUNDED

Over 3,000 men used to work in Penrhyn quarry at the end of the 19C; today it attracts visitors who enjoy the thrill over flying over it on the zipwire.

Tourism

Tourists have been coming to Wales for centuries. They came in coaches or on horseback in the 18C, to wonder at the mountains and the waterfalls. By the end of that century some would also venture here to see the new industries that were changing the landscape of Wales – and the world. Wales was the first country in the world to be industrialized.

Later on in the 19C, families began to come to the spa towns and the seaside villages. This is why there are so many houses from that time in Llandrindod and Llanwrtyd, and in Tenby, Aberystwyth and Llandudno.

Nant Gwrtheyrn in Llŷn used to be a quarrying village. Then the quarry closed and the people left. Then things changed again – a centre was set up there to teach Welsh, and the village is busy again.

Some people still visited the mountains too, and this is when people began climbing them. Mountain climbing became popular in that century.

Tourists still come to the beaches and lakes of Wales today, and climb the hills and walk the footpaths. Their equipment and their way of travelling are new, although the landscape is so old. Many people come to find out about the culture of Wales too, going to eisteddfodau and folk festivals. Those first tourists were amazed by the metal furnaces, and the towering cliffs where the quarrymen would work the slate. These places still attract tourists, because some of them are museums now and others offer the thrill of flying on a zipwire above an old quarry.

The history of the Welsh language is one of the wonders of Wales. It is one of the oldest languages in Europe. Thousands of children are educated in Welsh, although so much was done to remove it from schools. Caradog and Buddug would recognise many Welsh words and there are children with their names in school here now.

More and more people are learning Welsh, and come here to learn or to practise the language. While some of the sites of the heavy industries have been turned into museums, one of them, the village of Nant Gwrtheyrn, has become a centre for people who want to learn Welsh.

The National Eisteddfod is a festival of the Welsh language and it is one of the main events in our calendar. You can see every side of Welsh life and culture there – and have a lot of fun as well.

Conclusion

History is all around us every day, in buildings and ruins, in paths and roads, and in the words of our language as well. You can ignore it, but it has made the world you live in, and you yourself are part of history now!

The Welsh football and rugby teams wear red shirts, and their fans like to stand together to watch a game, wearing red shirts and waving their banners. They are the Red Wall of Wales. I like to think of the people who used to live and work in the buildings you can see in this book as the Invisible Red Wall. Every one of them would be waving a banner – St David's, or Glyndŵr's, or a banner asking for the People's Charter or Votes for Women. Do you have a place in the Red Wall? And what banner would you choose?

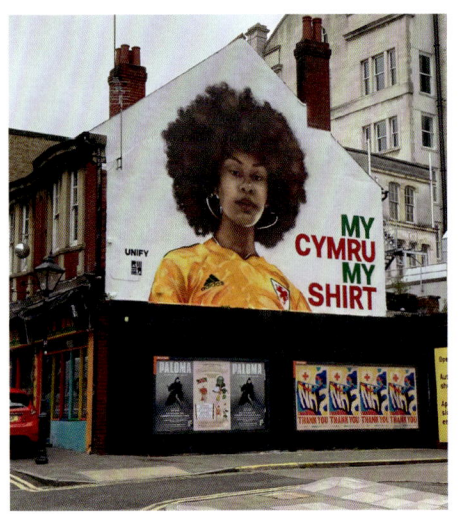

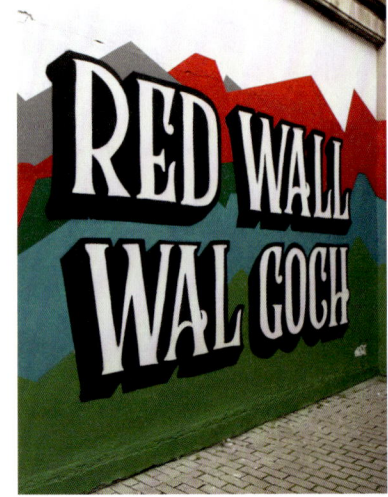

Murals in Cardiff during the Euro football tournament, 2021

A MYSTERY IN THE GROUND

The iron slave chain discovered at Llyn Cerrig Bach

Links of the past

In 1943 a piece of land was being cleared in order to extend the airfield at Valley, Anglesey. William Owen Roberts noticed that the workers were using an unusual chain to pull a tractor out of the mud. This chain wasn't one of the tools they were supposed to use. When he looked at it more closely, he saw that it was very old, although the links had been made stronger with a modern technique of pinching each one in the middle. He took a photograph of the chain and sent it to the National Museum.

The head of the archaeological department went straight up to Anglesey. He knew that the chain had been made 2,000 years ago. He arranged for the ground to be cleared carefully, and all the treasures of Llyn Cerrig Bach came to light again.

But even today nobody knows how or why the secret of making links stronger was lost for over a thousand years ...

HISTORY GROUNDED

End of the last Ice Age
-12000

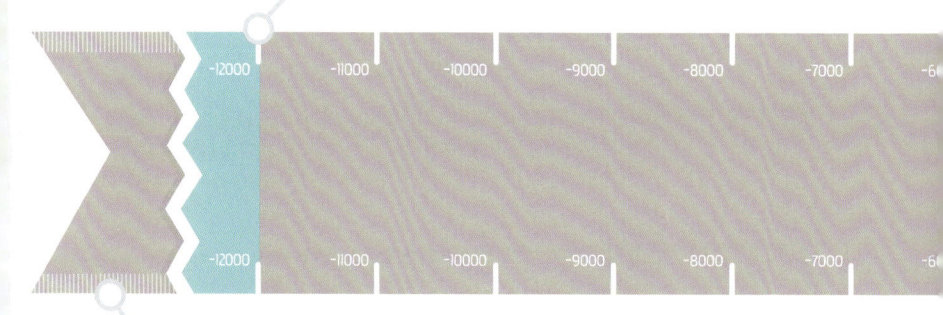

| -12000 | -11000 | -10000 | -9000 | -8000 | -7000 |

The Stone Age
-230000

The End of the Stone Age about -3300

HISTORY GROUNDED

The Iron Age from about -700

The Digital Revolution from about 1990 onwards

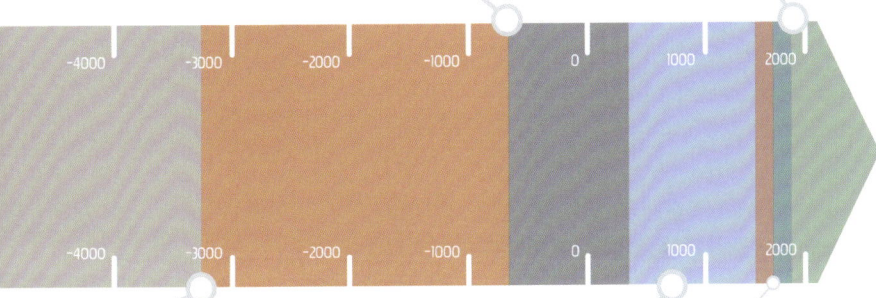

The Bronze Age

The Age of Revolutions

The Middle Ages

HISTORY GROUNDED

Measuring time

History is being made every day. And the world is changing all the time. Sometimes big changes happen suddenly because of war or disease. But life usually changes slowly for us, and so does the world around us. And we put labels on the different periods of this history.

When we look back over our lives, we like to put labels on the different parts of our own history. We say, "When I was a baby ... When I was seven ..." and so on. You will hear older people saying, "When I learnt to drive ..." or "When I was living in ..." We use labels like this when we look back at the history of our world too. Here are some of them.

Early Times

"Early Times" is one label on the years long, long ago, and it describes hundreds of thousands of years. Because of this, we put labels on different periods of these Early Times.

We usually talk about the time before people like us came to live in Europe as the "**Ice Ages**", because for long periods much of the ground was hidden under layers of ice and snow. At other times the weather would get better and it would be possible for animals and people to live here.

It was during one of those times when the weather was quite good that people were living in the cave at Pontnewydd, St Asaph. Today, we only have the things they left behind at the very back of the cave: the snow and ice came back to sweep everything else away. The last Ice Age came to an end about 20,000 years ago.

As the climate got better, and the ice retreated further and further to the north, people and animals came back to live here. And this is the beginning of a series of labels now. We call the time when people only used stone tools the "**Stone Age**". When they began to use metals like copper and tin, this is the start of the "**Bronze Age**".

Once people learnt how to make iron, then we use the label "**Iron Age**" for those years. And we are living in the Iron Age today – think of all the metal things there are in your home. They are made of steel, but steel is made from iron.

Because the people of those times didn't write, another label on the Early Times is "Pre-history" – before there is any written evidence for people's lives.

The Time of the Celts and Romans

The Celts and the Romans were the first people in Europe to use iron. The Celts lived all across Europe 4,000 years ago – this is the "**Age of the Celts**".

But Roman soldiers led by Julius Caesar began to take their lands from them about 2,000 years ago. Eventually, almost all of Britain became part of the Roman Empire, in spite of all Caradog and Boudicca's struggles.

The Romans brought the idea of writing to Britain, and so "history" is the label we give to their times and the periods that follow it.

But at the beginning of the 5C the soldiers of Rome weren't able to defend their Empire against the attacks of people from the north-east of Europe, like the Alemanni, the Franks – and the Saxons who started to make their homes in the east of Britain.

The Age of the Saints and the Dark Ages

The centuries between the beginning of the 5C and the 10C were troubled years of fighting. But these are the years when the old kingdoms of Wales were formed – the kingdoms which have given their names to parts of Wales today. And this is the period too when the Welsh saints were living – the saints who have given their names to so many towns and villages in Wales. Christianity had come to Wales with the Romans, and Welsh people had kept to that faith when other parts of Britain had forgotten it.

This is an important period in our history because it is now that we can begin to talk about Wales as a separate country. In Roman times, Wales and England were just one part of their empire, and there was no obvious difference between them. But Wales takes shape in the **Age of the Saints** as the princes defend their borders. This is the time when Offa's Dyke was built.

People used to call this period **"The Dark Ages"** because there is so little firm evidence for what was happening. But we are finding out more and more about these years, so this name is becoming more and more inaccurate.

The Age of the Princes and the Middle Ages

In the 10C strong leaders like Hywel Dda and Gruffudd ap Llywelyn were beginning to unite the different kingdoms of Wales. Then the Normans won the Battle of Hastings in 1066, and started to attack Wales soon after. Between 1066 and 1282 the princes of Wales tried to defend themselves against the Normans – sometimes by fighting them, and sometimes by making agreements with them.

In Wales, the label we use for this period is **"The Age of the Princes"** because we have so much information about the leaders of Wales at this time, and they were independent princes. There are lots of exciting stories about this time when every part of Wales had its own royal family.

But the Age of the Princes is different from all the other ages, because it ends very suddenly, and on one particular day. When Llywelyn ap Gruffudd was killed at Cilmeri, Powys, on 11 December 1282, the independence of Wales came to an end, and so did the Age of the Princes. Welsh people realised this at the time, and were very sad about it.

Another label on the time between 1000 and 1500 is **"The Middle Ages"** because when people started to put labels on the different periods of history, they thought these years came in the middle, between the Early Times and the modern world. It's quite a useful label when we talk about this period, because although the way Wales was ruled had changed in 1282, the way people live didn't change that much. Owain Glyndŵr wasn't a prince, but when he began his revolt, many people followed him because he was descended from the princes of Gwynedd and Powys.

The Age of the Tudors and the Early Modern Period

Henry Tudor's victory at the battle of Bosworth in 1485 is another turning point in the history of Wales, and of England too. It would be Henry and members of his family who would rule both countries from now on. His son, Henry VIII, made Wales part of England by the Acts of Union of 1536 and 1543. When James, king of Scotland, Henry VII's great-great-grandson, became King of England too in 1603 and made those two countries one, Wales was part of his new kingdom.

But the battle of Bosworth in 1485 wasn't the only important thing to happen at the end of the 15C. This was an important time of change and discovery in the history of Europe. In that century the printing press was invented, and some adventurous sailors reached America. These events opened the way for more inventions and discoveries. These are the foundations of our modern world, and the label that is put on the years between 1450 and 1700 is "**The Early Modern Period**".

This is the time when the Catholic Church lost its status as the only Christian church in Europe. Many people had criticised it before, but in 1507 Martin Luther began an argument against it which led to a time of bitter religious wars. But the end of the authority of the Catholic Church is also a step towards the modern world.

The Age of Revolutions

From 1700 things begin to change faster and in a lot of different ways. Science and technology developed, and every new discovery and invention led to more changes. People start to experiment with new ways of farming and with new crops, like potatoes, which came to Europe from America in the 17C.

People experimented too with new ways of making products like iron. New machines were invented, and a new form of power was discovered – steam. The label on this period is "**The Age of Revolutions**" because so many changes happen from 1700 onwards. Some people also talk about "The Agricultural Revolution" and "The Industrial Revolution" when they are describing the changes in farming and in industry, but these changes happened at the same time and for the same reasons.

But there is another reason for giving the label "Age of Revolutions" to the period 1700. In those years there were revolutions against the government in America and in France. First in America the people rebelled against the King of England, and won their independence in 1776. Then, in 1789, the people of France rebelled against their king. The king of France was executed in 1793, and there was a war in France for years afterwards.

The Victorian Age and the 19C

Victoria was queen from 1837 to 1901, and many people use her name as a label on the whole century from 1800 to 1900. This is the time when Britain became a very powerful industrial country, and won an empire which covered a large part of the world.

This is also a century when there were lots of protests against injustices in society, and by 1900 many improvements had been made in education, cleanliness in towns, safety at work and so on.

The Century of Ordinary People

During the 20C ordinary people start to have much more influence, are respected more, and have more of a voice in decisions which affect them. All men – and some women – got the right to vote in 1918, and every woman in 1928. Women and men who had been factory workers and miners became Members of Parliament. The unions which protect the rights of workers became very powerful. Everyone could have free education and health care. Changes in science and technology came faster and faster in the last century too.

The Plastic Age? The Time of the Computer? The Period of Climate Crisis?

You, the reader of this book, will decide what kind of age yours will be – and the label that's put on it too perhaps. Our history is in your hands from now on!

But remember – these labels are all ones we use when we are talking about the history of Europe. Many countries in the world have a much longer history than European countries do, and they have different labels on the periods of their history as well.

Image Sources

The publishers wish to gratefully acknowledge all assistance in obtaining permission to reproduce images from the following sources:

Alamy
191

The Author
8, 63, 146, 158, 177

The British Library
94 (Flickr commons)

CADW
30 (Crown Copyright (2021), Cadw, Image by Brian Byron, 82 (Crown Copyright (2021) Cadw, Image by Terry Ball)

Cambria
44

Cathays Heritage Library
171

Clwyd-Powys Archaeological Trust / GCG
21

Crown Copyright: RCAHMW
23, 31, 39, 61, 87,
30, 35 (copyright Paul R Davis)

Crown Copyright: Visit Wales
24, 25 (6), 27 (2), 31, 32 (2), 33, 34, 35 (2), 36, 43, 45, 49, 51 (2), 53, 57, 68, 70, 72 (2), 73, 74 (2), 75, 76 (3), 78, 79, 82, 84, 87, 89, 91, 95 (4), 96, 105 (2), 107, 113, 120, 127, 129, 145, 146, 148, 150, 152, 158, 164, 169, 176, 178, 187, 194, 196, 197 (2), 199 (2), 200, 202, 203, 204 (2), 220

Dafydd Elfryn
2

Dan Santillo
23

Dave Rendle (teifidancer)
119

Fferm a Thyddyn
198

Flickr
114 (netNicholls)

Football Association of Wales
203

Geograph
173 (Jaggery CC BY-SA-2.0)

Google Earth
84, 101, 125

Gwasg Carreg Gwalch
8, 9 (3), 10, 13, 14, 17, 26, 33, 38, 43 (University of Bangor Museum), 46 (2), 48, 50, 53, 58, 59, 60, 61, 67, 70, 71, 73 (Image by Chris Iliff), 75 (Image by Chris Iliff), 77 (2), 81, 81 (Image by Chris Iliff), 86, 89, 90 (2), 94, 106, 108, 109 (3), 113, 117, 126 (2), 129, 130, 131 (2), 132, 134 (2), 135, 137, 139 (2), 141, 143 (photograph: Sygun Copper Mine), 146, 147, 149 (2), 151 (2), 152, 155, 157 (2), 158, 159, 160 (2), 161, 162, 168, 170 (3), 172, 174 (2), 182 (2), 185, 188, 189 (2), 190 (2), 192 (3), 193, 199, 200, 202, 206 (2)

via Gwynfor Evans family
187 (Ken Davies)

Iestyn Hughes
16, 20, 26, 37, 53, 54, 63 (2), 71, 87, 111, 118, 121 (3), 134, 139, 155, 159, 170, 174 (2), 177, 179 (2), 182 (2), 183, 184, 191, 193, 195, 197, 203

John Meirion Morris, and Y Lolfa, from *The Celtic Vision*, with thanks to Gwawr Morris
27

Julian Heath
21, 22, 24

Keith O'Brien/GCG
185

Llanw Llŷn
134, 172

Marian Delyth
92

Mirrorpix
15, 173, 175, 176, 201

National Eisteddfod of Wales
205

The National Library of Wales
179, 186, 193 (Ray Daniel collection)

The National Library of Wales (Wikimedia Commons)
14, 16, 55, 62, 85, 88, 90, 91, 93, 98, 101, 102 (2), 103, 104 (2), 108, 109, 115, 116, 117, 119, 125, 127, 131, 132, 133, 138, 139, 142, 144, 152, 178, 179, 181, 193, 194, 195

The National Museum of Wales
27, 207

Newport Museum and Art Gallery
153, 165

New York Public Library
115 (George Arents collection)

Old Merthyr Tydfil (alangeorge.co.uk)
132

Pxhere.com
209

Radical Tea Towel
149

Rhys Mwyn / GCG
11 (2), 56 (2)

St Fagans National Museum of History
80 (2), 110, 172

Simon Evans
128

Snowdonia National Park
12

Tata Steel, Trostre
145

Trustees of the British Museum
39 (CC BY NC-SA 4.0)

Urdd Gobaith Cymru
188 (4),

Wikimedia
58 (Gareth James), 60 (FU), 71 (Richard Croft), 89 (Llywelyn2000), 208 (Luca Galuzzi)

Wikimedia Commons
40, 41 (Paul Walter), 42 (Kev Griffin), 42 (Alan Simkins), 46 (Llywelyn2000), 48 (Gareth James), 60 (PC), 83 (PC), 97 (2 PC), 107 (Seth Whales), 111 (Eirian Evans), 112 (Ham II), 139 (Pauline Eccles), 140 (Oxyman), 163 (PC), 175 (IWM PC), 181 (Ben Brooksbank), 196 (Russ Hamer)

Women's Archive Wales
154

Brief Index

Aber-arth	139
Aberaeron	179
Aberconwy	42
Aberdaron	84
Aberfan	191
Abergavenny	163, 165
Aberglasney, mansion	95
Aberystwyth	108, 133, 174, 179, 180, 189, 193, 204
America	116–117, 172
Amlwch, harbour	117
Arthur, king	58
Australia	153, 172
Bach-y-graig	103, 104
Bala	178
Bangor	160, 180, 202
Bangor-on-Dee	55
Barry	146, 159
Bassaleg	87
Bassey, Shirley	15
Beasley, Eileen	190, 200
Beaumaris, castle	76, 103
Beddgelert	143
Bersham	126
Berwyn, mountains	60
Bethesda	135, 144, 158
Betws-y-coed	182
Bevan, Aneurin	176–177
Big Pit	146
Black Bart	135
Blackwood	152
Blaenau Ffestiniog	137, 145, 158
Blaenavon	125, 143
Bodysgallen, mansion	95
Borth	20
Borth-y-gest	134
Brecon	30
Brecon Beacons	59
Britannia bridge	182
Brittany	133
Brochfael Ysgithrog	50
Bryn Cader Faner	25
Bryntail	145
Bryn-mawr	173
Buddug (Boudicca)	40, 41
Builth Wells	154
Bute Town	158
Bwlch Maen Gwynedd	60
Bwlch y Ddeufaen	43
Cadfarch	21
Caer Caradog	39
Caerleon	34–36, 43, 44
Caernarfon	33, 34, 36, 91
Caernarfon, castle	74, 76
Caerphilly	63, 203
Caerphilly, castle	75
Caerwent	32, 36
Calvin, John	98
Campbell, Betty	201
Capel Celyn	179
Caradog (Caratacus)	38, 39
Cardi Bach, the	180, 181
Cardiff	112, 146, 147, 169–171, 175, 177, 182, 194–195, 201, 202, 203
Cardiff Bay	169, 187, 188, 194, 195, 202
Cardiff, castle	73
Cardigan	181, 199
Carmarthen	42, 192
Carreg Cennen, castle	74
Carreg Samson	25
Castell Henllys	27
Castlemartin	174
Celts, the	28–32, 36–38
Cenarth	139
Chartists, the	150–153, 206
Chepstow, castle	72, 74
Chirk, castle	104, 105
Cilmeri	70, 71
Clough, Richard	103, 104
Clwyd, Ann	60
Coleg Cymraeg	189
Columbus, Christopher	97, 114
Constantine	32, 44
Conwy	116, 96
Corwen	89, 120
Crawshay, Richard	135, 143
Crusades	79, 88
Cwm Taf	191
Cwm-hir, abbey	121
Cwmtudu	133, 134
Cwmystwyth	128, 129, 145
Cyfarthfa	135, 143, 150
Cymdeithas yr Iaith	192–193
Cynddylan	54
Dafydd ap Gwilym	87
Davies, Gwilym	183
Dee, river	59
Denbigh	101, 172
Din Llugwy	25

Dinas Dinlle	11	Hywel ap Cadell	
Dinas Emrys	58	(Hywel Dda)	62, 63
Dinefwr, castle	72		
Dinorwig quarry	144	Ifan ab Owen Edwards	188
Dolaucothi	42, 145	Ifor ap Meurig (Ifor Bach)	73, 80
Dolbadarn, castle	72, 74	Iolo Goch	86
Drws-y-coed	145	Iolo Morganwg	119
Dyfi, river	59	Ireland	133, 159
		Isaac, Norah	189
Ebbw Vale	176, 181	Isle of Man	133
Edward I	70, 71, 74, 76	Iwan, Dafydd	190
Efail-wen	151		
Efyrnwy, reservoir	178	Jones, Berwyn	60
Eglwysilan	63	Jones, Griffith	161
Elizabeth I	105, 125		
Epynt, Mynydd	109, 174, 186	Katheryn of Berain	103, 104
Esgair Hir	128		
Evans, Dic	200	Labour Party	176
Evans, Gwynfor	186–187	Lampeter	193
		Laws of Hywel Dda, the	62, 63, 85, 92, 99
Felinheli	138	Little Garth	42
Ffos-y-ffin	60, 61	Little Newport	135
Fishguard	159	Liverpool	178–179
Frost, John	152–153	Llanbedr-goch	56
		Llancaeach Fawr, mansion	95
George, David Lloyd	168, 169, 171, 175	Llandaf	194
George, Megan Lloyd	186	Llandeilo Tal-y-bont	110
Gerald of Wales	73, 79	Llandovery	109
Glyndyfrdwy	120	Llandrillo-yn-Rhos	46
Gower	23	Llandrindod	154, 155
Graig Lwyd	24	Llandudno	42, 182
Great Orme	42	Llanelli	189, 190
Griffiths, Ann	118	Llanfaglan	45
Gruffudd ap Cynan	77, 78	Llanfihangel-yng-Ngwynfa	1118
Gruffudd ap Llywelyn	67	Llanfoist	165
Gutenburg, Johann	97	Llanfyllin	157
Gwenllian (daughter		Llangennech	190
of Gruffudd)	71, 80	Llangollen	131
Gwenllian (daughter		Llangrannog	188
of Llywelyn)	70, 71	Llangybi	51
Gwerful Mechain	92–94	Llanidloes	107, 151
Gwydir, mansion	95, 103	Llannefydd	104
		Llanrhaeadr-yng-	
Halkyn Moutain	126, 145	Nghinmeirch	111
Harlech, castle	74, 90, 91	Llanrwst	131, 157, 182
Hay-on-Wye	108	Llanthony, priory	84
Hedd Wyn	12, 170	Llanwenog	54
Heledd, lament	54	Llanwrtyd	154
Henry Tudor (Henry VII)	86, 94, 96, 97, 103, 105	Llanymynech	132
Henry VIII	97–100, 105, 111, 160	Llwynypia	148
Holyhead	159, 196	Llŷn	30
Holyhead Mountain	27	Llyn Cerrig Bach	207
Hopwood, Mererid	92	Llyn Fawr	27

Llyn Tegid	178	Owain Glyndŵr	13, 86, 87, 89–91, 120–121, 206
Llyn y Fan Fach	24		
Llys Rhosyr	80	Painscastle	72
Llywelyn ap Gruffudd (Llywelyn Ein Llyw Olaf)	70, 71, 74, 75	Pandy Tudur	138
		Parys, Mountain	126, 127, 143, 145
Llywelyn ap Iorwerth (Llywelyn Fawr)	70	Patrishow church	111
		Paviland Cave	22, 23
Luther, Martin	98	Peace Petition	183
		Pembroke Dock	159
Machynlleth	59, 89, 90	Pembroke, castle	78, 94
Mackworth, Sir Humphrey	128	Pen-y-crug	30
Maen Achwyfan	55	Penbryn	37
Maen Beuno	46	Penmaen-mawr	24, 27
Maen Llia	10	Penmon	51
Maen Penfras Uchaf	25	Penmynydd, mansion	94
Maesyronnen	113	Pennal	89, 90
Mawddach, estuary	174	Pennant Melangell	50
Melin Gruffudd	138	Pennant, Thomas	85
Melin Llynnon	139	Penrhyn quarry	135, 144, 204
Merthyr Tudful	135, 140–144, 149, 150	Pentre Ifan	25
Miles, Elizabeth	154	Pentreuchaf	162
Milford Haven	196, 197	Penyberth	185
Moelfre	200	Pilleth, battle	13
Mold	202	Plaid Cymru	186, 187, 192
Morgan, Bishop William	102	Plas Mawr, mansion	96, 105
Morgan, Henry	135	Pontarddulais	145, 151
Morris, John Meirion	27	Pontcysyllte	132
Mostyn	125	Pontio Arts Centre	202
Mynydd Gorddu	197	Pontnewydd Cave	21
		Pontypridd	63, 154, 155, 164
Nanhoron	113	Pope, the	32, 97, 110, 114
Nant Gwrtheyrn	204	Porth Ysgaden	134
Nant-y-glo	164	Preseli, hills	26, 184
Nantgarw, pottery	132	Presteigne	131
National Eisteddfod	171, 205	Prion	198
National Museum of History, St Fagans	80, 107, 110	Pwllheli	117, 162, 180
National Museum of Wales	195, 207	Radio Cymru/Radio Wales	202
National Parks, the	198	Rebecca Riots	151
National Theatre Wales	202	Recorde, Robert	114
National Waterfront Museum	140	Red Dragon, the	58
		Red Wall of Wales, the	206
Neath	127, 128	Rhiw	172
Nelson	203	Rhondda Heritage Park	197
Nest (daughter of Rhys)	78, 92	Rhondda Valley	154, 159
Nevern	46	Rhosllannerchrugog	146
Newcastle Emlyn	184	Rhuddlan, castle	74, 76, 77
Newport	146, 151, 152–153, 165	Rhulen	48
Normans, the	68–78	Rhyl	189
		Rhymney Valley	60
Oakeley quarry	145	Rhys ap Tewdwr	78
Offa's Dyke	52–54, 188	Rhys, lord	70, 86
Ogham, alphabet	54	Richard, Henry	183

Rogers, Samuel Baldwyn	164, 165	Tregaron	183
Romans, the	32–43, 44, 45	Treuddyn	188
Rosebush	158	Trevithick, Richard	140
		Tryweryn	178–179, 186
		Tudors, the	94, 96, 102, 107
S4C	202	Tŷ Mawr, Wybrnant	103
Sarn Elen	42	Tywyn	138
Savery, Thomas	140		
Scotland	133	Urdd Gobaith Cymru	188, 189
Senedd Cymru	147, 186–187	Uwchmynydd	84
Senghennydd	73, 80, 147, 200		
Severn Bridge	164	Valle Crucis, abbey	82
Severn, river	59	Vikings, the	56, 57
Skokholm	57	Votes for Women	171, 206
Skomer	57	Vulcana	163
slavery	115–117, 135		
Snowdon	199	Wales Millennium Centre	202
Snowdonia	67	Welsh Not	161
Speed, John	101	Welsh Slate Museum	197
St Asaph	21	White Castle	68
St Brynach's cross	46	White, Rawlins	112
St Cybi	51	Willliam the Conqueror	68
St David	47–49, 206	Wiston, castle	72
St David's	48, 49, 79	World War II	173–175, 180
St Melangell	50	World War I	168–170, 200
St Non's chapel	49	Wrexham	130, 142
St Patrick	49		
St Seiriol	51	Ysgol Dewi Sant	189
Stepaside	129	Ysgol Glan Clwyd	189
Stonehenge	26	Ysgol Gynradd Gymraeg Hamadryad	15
Strata Florida, abbey	82	Ysgol Lluest	189
Swansea	132, 140, 146, 159, 173, 192, 202, 203	Ysgol Rhiwddolion	17
Swyddffynnon	139	Ysgwrn	12
Sycharth	87, 90		
Sygun	143		
Tacitus	38		
Tal-y-llyn	27		
Tal-y-sarn	158		
Tenby	105		
Theatr Clwyd	202		
Thomas, Helen	184		
Tiger Bay	15, 169		
Tinkinswood	25		
Tintern, abbey	82		
Tomen y Mur	35		
Tonypandy	138		
Trawsfynydd	170, 185		
Tre'r Ceiri	30		
Tredegar	176		
Trefechan, bridge	193		
Trefforest	164		
Tre-fin	139		